A CALL TO DESTINY

THE CALL OF THE ROSE SERIES
BOOK TWO

BY

CHANELLE NASH

For my Mum and Daddy
Love you both loads

Chapter One

Jessica walked up the dark path towards the six-bedroom house that had been in her family for generations. Tall sycamore trees lined the path on one side and horse-chestnut trees lined the other. The trees were centuries old, all of which were overgrown. They gave the path an eerie look to it during the day light hours and at night it was just down right spooky.

Why she decided to wait until the evening to come to the house, she didn't know. It had always scared her to walk the path, which was more like a long drive-way. Memories flooded her mind taking her back to when she was younger with her brother and two sisters playing along the path near the house. They use to collect conkers or try to catch the fruit from the sycamore as it fell from the tree like helicopters.

Jessica looked up at the house as she walked steadily closer to it. She could hear the squelch of the wet leaves under her knee high black leather boots. Her blue jeans were getting wet in the process. There had always been at least one family member living in the house at all times. The last resident was her Great Uncle Theodore who had recently passed away. Jessica's brother Jordan, who was five years older than her had been in the process of moving into the house before their uncle, but nothing had come of it. In fact, she didn't even know what had happened to her brother. He had one day just disappeared. It was like he had vanished off the face of the earth. Her mother had said not to worry about it that he probably just needed some time to himself.

She pushed the thought of her brother out of her mind as she made it to the front door. Hunting around in her hand bag for what seemed like forever, she finally found the keys. Looking up at the white painted door, she took note of the stained-glass window with a picture of a rose bud in it. Jessica looked at the rose with a puzzled expression. She could have sworn the rose was in bloom the last time she saw it. Shrugging it off as a mistaken childhood memory she opened the door.

Jessica stood in the middle of what you would think was a grand entrance to a mansion. It had changed a lot since she had last been there. The once polished wooden floor now looked to be made of marble. Tilting her head up toward the ceiling, there as she remembered, was a sparkling crystal chandelier. To complete the ambiance of the room there was a beautifully polished grand staircase. Matching bannisters lined the stairs and ran all the way around an open hall way. Jessica remembered coming out of her designated bedroom many times and peering over the railing and into the hall below.

She glanced around at her surroundings. To her left was the archway to the living room and directly opposite was an archway to the dining room and large kitchen. Looking at the floor of the entrance, Jessica guessed her Uncle had done some renovating. She got quite excited about discovering what else had been changed within the house. Yawning loudly into the empty room Jessica decided she would investigate after she had gotten some sleep. It had been a long train ride from Scotland.

Chucking her ruck sack on her back, she headed up the stairs to the room that had always been hers when she stayed.

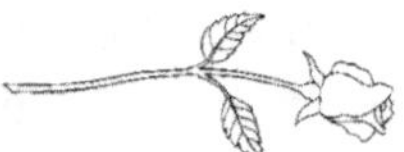

Jessica woke a short time later to the song 'Hungry like the Wolf.' Looking over at the bed side table she grabbed her mobile phone to answer it.

"Rise and shine sleepy head." It was Jessica's best friend Charlotte.

"I'm up, but I refuse to shine," Jessica replied rubbing her eyes.

"That's my girl, always a grumpy bum in the mornings. I take it you got to the mansion alright then?"

"It's not a mansion," Jessica said bluntly to her friend.

"You keep telling yourself that darling. I've been there, remember? The place is like the bloody Tardis. It looks like a two-story cottage on the outside, but go inside and it's a small mansion," teased Charlotte. "Any way I will be leaving the flat in an hour to get to your Tardis— I mean Mansion—I mean…. ah stuff it your ancestral home. So, I will see you soon," chuckled Charlotte.

"You've been watching Doctor Who again haven't you?" It wasn't really a question. Jessica knew she had been.

"Well yeah. Always," Charlotte said with a laugh.

"Don't forget my boys, I haven't seen them in a week," Jessica said before her friend could hang up.

"Well that's what happens when you work away. Don't worry, I won't forget the boys. It's going to be fun trying to get two Alsatians to sit still while I drive down the motorway. I just hope they will fit in my car," Charlotte replied.

"I'm sure you will work something out, see you when you get here."

Jessica hung up the phone, giggling to herself. She could imagine her friend trying to get Fane and Decebel into the mini. She had named them after her favourite characters in a book series which she had been reading when she gotten them.

She sat up in her four-poster double bed, getting reacquainted with the old room. Looking around she realised it hadn't changed at all from when she was there six years ago, her grandparents had still been alive then and the room looked exactly how she had remembered it. Lilac velvet curtains hung on the windows over some lace curtains which had fairies on them. The walls had dark purple wall paper on the bottom half and were painted lilac on the top half. A white boarder of velvet spirals separated the two halves. She smiled as she noticed the Duran Duran posters that were still spread throughout the room. Most of the posters she noticed were of John Taylor and Simon Le Bon.

"Ten points for guessing who my favourites are," she said as she climbed out of bed.

Emerging from the bathroom sometime later, Jessica checked her watch. She still had a little bit of time before Charlotte would arrive. So, with that in mind she headed down to the kitchen to make a coffee. She decided to grab her ruck sack as she left the room.

When she walked into the kitchen she found most of it had changed. The kitchen counters were now what looked like marble and the floor had pearl coloured tiles. The cupboards had black acrylic doors and the appliances were all black to match.

"Very posh," she thought aloud.

Placing her ruck sack on the counter she proceeded to take out the coffee, milk and sugar she had grabbed on her way to the house. She had grabbed it just in case there was no food in the house when she got there. Opening the fridge and cupboards as she went she was surprised to find that they were full of food and all of it was fresh. She guessed her parents had been at the house quite recently. Her mother always liked to leave the cupboards full. Putting the kettle on, she pulled her phone out of her pocket and dialled.

"Hello?" a voice answered on the second ring.

"Hey Mum, how have you and Dad been?" Jessica asked.

"We're good sweetheart," her mother replied.

"That's good….um mum, have you been to Rose Manor lately?"

There was a pause for a minute before her mother asked. "Why?"

"Well the cupboards are full and —"

"You're at the house?" her mother asked cutting her off. Her voice had a note of panic in it.

"Yeah, I told you I was going to be moving here when we spoke at Uncle Theodore's funeral," Jessica said as she put the coffee and sugar into her Cliff Richard mug. "Is there a problem with me living here?"

There was another long pause. "No sweetheart I just didn't think it would be so soon. Are you there on your own?" her mother asked remembering what happened with Jordan.

"At the moment I am. Charlotte is on her way up here with my boys."

"That's good. How long will Charlotte be staying?" she asked sounding relieved.

"A couple of days at the moment but that could change, you know how she hates being on her own."

"Yep. Your father and I have seen quite a lot of her this week while you've been in Scotland."

Jessica laughed. It didn't surprise her to hear that. The flat that she shared with Charlotte in London was a fifteen-minute walk from her parent's house.

"So, what do you girls plan on doing for the day?" her mother asked.

"Well I was going to do some food shopping but the cupboards are all full. We still might head to the shops any way to get some stuff for Fane and Decebel. It all depends on if Charlotte forgets to bring anything with her," Jessica replied.

"Sounds like fun. So, what fun stuff have you got planned for tonight?"

"Oh, you know us eat lots of popcorn and chocolate while washing it down with coke and watching gorgeous hunky guys on TV."

"So, a normal night for you two then," her mother replied, laughing.

"Pretty much," Jessica replied with a sigh. "Have you heard from Jordan at all?" she asked changing the subject.

"No sweetie. Don't worry I'm sure he will be home soon."

"You have been saying that since he disappeared."

"He didn't disappear," her mother said sternly.

"Yeah right! Nobody but you and Dad have heard from him in five years."

"He has a lot of soul searching to do."

"I'll give him soul searching, next time I see him."

"I bet you will," her mother said chuckling to herself.

"Mum, I'm sorry to cut this short but I really have to go."

"So soon?" she asked, surprised.

"I really need a pee."

"Oh, alright then. I had better let you go, love you."

"Love you too." With that, Jessica hung up the phone and bolted up the stairs.

Chapter Two

"She's just a devil woman with evil on her mind, beware -" Jessica sung to the empty house.

"Stop singing that crap," said a voice through the letter box.

With a big smile on her face Jessica opened the front door. She replied looking at her friend, "Don't you dare be dissing the Cliff man."

Charlotte feigned shock as she placed her hand on her chest and replied, "As if I would."

Giggling at her friend, Jessica pulled her into a tight embrace. Suddenly Jessica and Charlotte were knocked over as Fane and Decebel tried to make a fuss of her. Smiling she stroked them both before climbing to her feet.

"So how was the drive?" she asked Charlotte.

"Fast. The motorway was clear although I did get some funny looks. I think that was mostly due to the fact I had two massive dogs in my small car."

"I don't know," Jessica said looking her friend over. "Have you seen what you're wearing? I mean that bright pink tank top. Its bloody freezing and you're wearing that. I am getting cold just looking at you."

Charlotte looked down at what she had chosen to wear that morning. White shorts and the above mentioned pink tank top. What had she been thinking? "I guess I was thinking of somewhere hot when I got dressed," she said half-heartedly.

"Or someone, knowing you," Jessica said leading them into the kitchen.

"Cheeky cow," Charlotte said looking back at the front door distractedly. "Didn't that rose have petals?"

When Jessica reached the kitchen, she threw the jumper which was hanging on the back of the chair to her friend on her way to open the back door to the garden to let her dogs out. Turning around she gasped when she noticed the jumper her friend had on. It belonged to her brother. Jessica was puzzled, she didn't understand how her brother's jumper came to be sitting on the back of the chair. Had he been there lately? Taking a closer look at the jumper, she realised it just so happened to be the jumper that Charlotte had given him. The one she gave to him at the Christmas before he went on his, "soul search," as their mother had put it. She was surprised Charlotte hadn't noticed.

"Wow, this room has hell changed since I was last here," Charlotte said rubbing her hands over the front of the jumper.

"I know right," Jessica replied heading to the kettle to make them a coffee. "I got here rather late last night so I haven't had a good look around yet. I was going to do that today but I thought I would wait until you got here knowing how nosey you can be sometimes."

"You know me so well. It will be like a little adventure," Charlotte said as a wicked grin crossed her face. Jessica could also see the calculating gleam of her eyes.

"No," Jessica said to her friend as she opened her mouth to say something.

"What?" said Charlotte stunned. "I didn't say anything."

"You were going to and the answer is no." Jessica knew which room her friend wanted to start with during their look around. Her heart sank at the look of sadness that crossed her friends face. Handing Charlotte the mug of coffee she had just made her she asked, "So which room would you like to stay in? Or is that a silly question." Jessica smiled as she watched her friends face light up. It really was a silly question.

The two women sat around the dining room table. Jessica giggled as she watched Charlotte wiggle her bum on the sheep skin chairs trying to get comfortable as if they weren't comfy enough to start with. Tracing shapes on the glass top table she watched her friend stare out the back door. If she knew Charlotte, she was no doubt staring at nothing when a dreamy look crossed her face. Charlotte always had a certain look come over her and Jessica knew straight away what or should she say whom her friend was thinking about. She had been so caught up with her own emotions about her brother leaving it had never occurred to her how his disappearance had affected Charlotte.

In that moment, Jessica felt like a really bad friend. She didn't deserve Charlotte as a friend. The look on her face said that wherever her thoughts had taken her, she was starting to get upset. Tapping her friends arm to get her attention she said, "You know what we need?"

"Chocolate," Charlotte automatically said.

"Chocolate, seriously?"

"What? I always need chocolate," Charlotte said innocently.

"Is that before or after the perve session that I have a planned?"

"What, not during?" Charlotte asked totally shocked at the prospect. "That's not going to be a good perve session. You can't have a good perve session without chocolate, ice cream, trifle, chocolate mousse, cake, oh and crisps," she mused while counting the items off on her fingers as she said them.

Jessica smiled at her friend.

"I knew that would work," she said mostly to herself.

"What would work?" Charlotte asked.

"Nothing," Jessica said smiling as she led her friend out of the room. "Come on you, let's go get the stuff out of the car before we get too comfortable in front of a nice warm fire and forget all about it."

Chapter Three

Jessica sat on a rug in the living room in front of the fireplace. A fire was crackling in the hearth which added a warm glow to the room. Leaning up against the settee she stroked Fane and Decebel who were lying on either side of her. Her best friend Charlotte was off to her left by the television laying on a blanket reading. "What are you reading?"

"There and Now," Charlotte replied. She tilted onto her side to show Jessica the front cover before lying back down on her stomach.

"Is it any good?" Jessica asked.

Without looking up from her book Charlotte replied, "Absolutely and that Jonathan Fortner, I would so have him."

"You are such a perve, you know that?" Jessica pointed out to her friend.

Charlotte sat up and faced her friend.

"I guess you didn't think that about those characters you named your dogs after."

"That's not the point," Jessica replied staring at the flames. She was avoiding the glare she knew her friend would be giving her.

"You just won't admit that you're just as big a perve as me," Charlotte said.

"If I am, it's only because you're a bad influence."

Charlotte's response was a laugh. "I got that Pink song in my head now, lordy, lordy, lordy I can't help it I like to party, it's genetic —"

"No, it's not," Jessica said interrupting her friend before she got the chance to get up and start dancing and singing at the top of her lungs. Extremely badly. "So, my friend who can't sing. What are we going to do tonight?"

"Watch Doctor Who," Charlotte replied with a big grin.

"Again, But we haven't long finished watching Doctor Who."

"I love Doctor Who."

"Ok then so which one…. Eccleston, Tennant or Smith?"

"Does it matter? I'd have all of them as well."

"In your dreams."

"Every night baby," Charlotte replied grinning like a Cheshire cat.

Jessica rolled her eyes at her friend. "How about we start off with the first episode and go from there?"

"Sounds good," Charlotte replied going back to reading her book.

Jessica decided to watch a bit of normal telly to pass the time, before the evenings Doctor Who marathon they were planning to have. They had already watched a couple of the episodes that had Jack in them. Jessica liked him so she wasn't complaining. Turning on the television with the remote, she started flicking channels.

"Oi, put that back," said Charlotte suddenly. Obviously, someone on a television show had caught her attention.

"What?" Jessica said startled. She hadn't even been paying attention to what was on the screen as she flicked the channels. Flicking the channel back, Jessica found the station Charlotte was referring too. "Power Rangers, are you kidding me?"

"What?" Charlotte said innocently.

"Please tell me why I currently have The Power Rangers blaring out of my television?"

"Tommy…. Duh," Charlotte said looking at her friend like she should know that already.

"You still like him?"

"Hell yeah, he is so yummy."

"You so need a boyfriend."

"Well if the object of my desire would notice me…."

"Let's not go there," Jessica said. She knew exactly who the object of her friend's desire was. Jessica thought it rather funny that Charlotte still hadn't realised she had that person's jumper on. If Jessica hadn't already gotten used to Charlottes behaviour where her brother was concerned she would be totally grossed out.

"That's it! Enough perve sessions for you. It's like you have a homing beacon or something," she said as she stood up and turned off the television.

Jessica couldn't help but smile at the disappointed look on her friends' face. She even had the pouty bottom lip happening.

"Come on let's go get some dinner sorted before we start on the junk food."

"Don't forget the chocolate," Charlotte said as she followed Jessica out the room.

Chapter Four

Jessica woke the next morning and smiled at her friend still sleeping next to her. It had been so late by the time they had finished watching their Doctor Who marathon they both decided to sleep in her bed like they did when they were younger and sort out a room for Charlotte in the morning. Jessica slowly pulled the covers off herself, climbed out of bed and headed to the bathroom.

Emerging sometime later showered and dressed she noticed that Charlotte was sitting up in the bed writing in her dream journal. "Was my brother invading your dreams again?"

Charlotte startled at Jessica's voice as she was so engrossed in writing she hadn't heard her come out of the bathroom. "Yep," she replied looking at her friend.

"Well going by the smile on your face, I'm guessing it was a good dream." She smiled as Charlotte nodded with a cheesy grin on her face. "I'm going to get breakfast started. I'll see you when you get down there," Jessica shouted over her shoulder as she left the room.

"I'll be down soon. I just have to finish writing this while I remember it," Charlotte said as she went back to her dream journal.

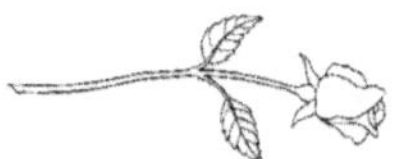

Jessica patted her stomach as she put the last dish away. She felt stuffed after the full English breakfast they had just polished off. She looked over at Charlotte sitting at the table. The look on her face said she was itching to get their house exploring started. Jessica couldn't blame her. Even though she knew the only room Charlotte cared about was Jordan's. As much as Jessica didn't want to go in there she couldn't pass up the chance. She had never been allowed in any of the other bedrooms except her parents or grandparents.

A devilish smile crossed her face when she thought Nanny wasn't here to stop her now. She looked over at Charlotte who was staring at the look on her face.

"What you smiling about?" Charlotte asked peering at her friend.

"I was just thinking. I actually get to fully explore this house," Jessica said while putting the kettle on.

"I know, what's your point?"

"My Nan aint here to stop me," Jessica replied, her grin getting even wider.

"Ah, I get it now," Charlotte replied as understanding dawned on her.

When she finished making their coffees Jessica picked up the cups and headed for the table. She placed the cups down and took the seat opposite her friend.

"So, which room should we start with?"

"How about the attic and work our way down," Charlotte suggested.

"What!" Jessica looked at her friend totally dumbfounded.

"You thought I was going to say Jordan's room. Didn't you?" Charlotte asked, pleased that she had totally stunned her friend.

"I did actually. I know you where my brother is concerned, you're obsessed."

"What can I say, he is the one that my heart has chosen. Besides I did think of Jordan's room first but then I figured, save the best till last," Charlotte explained with a big smile on her face.

"I knew there was a catch to it," Jessica said with a smile. "Come on, let's get this party started," she said while polishing off the last of her coffee.

When Jessica reached the top of the house she opened the door to the attic. At first glance she felt like she was about to walk onto the set of Charmed. As she ventured further into the room she noticed that it seemed to be divided. One side had the usual old family items that were stored away in the wooden cabinets along the wall. That side of the room looked rather new as if the cabinets were a recent addition.

The other side of the room had the complete opposite feel and look to it. There were display cabinets that had glass doors that slid across. Different shaped jars and containers were on the shelves. Off to the side was a table with a small camp stove that had a large black bowl on it. Vials and small perfume bottles were placed neatly on the table away from the bowl. Jessica's attention was drawn to the large book stand that resembled the ones the bible sat on in church. A very large leather bound book sat closed on the stand. She headed straight for it as curiosity got the better of her.

"What is this?" she asked. She held the book up to show Charlotte.

"That would be a grimoire."

"A what?" Jessica said as she placed the book back on its resting place.

"A grimoire, commonly known as a book of shadows."

"And what the hell is that when it's at home?"

"It's a spell book," Charlotte answered giving Jessica a puzzled look. "Did we watch the same charmed episodes or were you too preoccupied with the blokes on the show?"

"But that's just a television show."

"Some parts of television shows are based on some fact or myth, like supernatural for example," Charlotte replied while heading to the cabinets with the jars on them.

"So why did you call the book of shadows a grimoire?"

"Because that's what it's called."

"How would you know?"

Charlotte looked at her friend. "What, you think I work in a new age shop and know nothing?"

"I thought you owned it."

"I do, but I still work there," Charlotte said looking at her friend like she was an idiot.

"I saw that look," Jessica said.

"Well don't say stupid things and you won't get my you're an idiot look," Charlotte responded as she resumed looking at the jars and containers. Jessica walked over to her friend.

"Ok smart arse, what are these for?" she asked motioning to the jars.

"The herbs are for… I'm guessing the spells in the book you were looking at."

"What no lambs heart, or newt's eyes?" Jessica asked sarcastically thinking this was all a big joke.

Charlotte gave her a filthy look. "No, that is dark magic. This all seems to be good magic."

"What's the difference?" Jessica asked with genuine curiosity.

"The purpose in which they are used for of course. Basically, dark magic is all about causing harm to someone and what benefits the spell has for the person casting it. It usually requires blood for the spell to succeed. Good magic is more like being in harmony with ones-self and everything around them. The magic is not used to harm anybody, it is used to heal. There is more to it but I will leave it at that for now," said Charlotte noticing the glazed look on her friend's face. "So, who is the witch in your family?"

"Stuffed if I know. I never knew this stuff was up here," Jessica replied. She spotted a large trunk under a rather picturesque arched window. "What do you think is in that?"

"In what?" Charlotte asked looking over to where her friend was headed. "I would think it's full of old documents, most probably on your family."

"Sweet, let's take a look." Jessica gathered up the trunk and examined it. "Blast it!" she said with frustration.

"What is it?" Charlotte asked.

"It's locked. We will just have to take it downstairs and have a look for the key later," Jessica said trying to get a better grip on the box. "And a key hole."

"Why not look for the key now?" Charlotte asked.

"If we find the key and there is interesting stuff in here, then we will get caught up with that and not finish our house exploring." Jessica said triumphantly.

"Good point. I didn't think of that," Charlotte said as she followed Jessica out the room.

Chapter Five

After exploring the other rooms which were usually off limits to them Jessica and Charlotte noticed that you could easily tell who they belonged to. 'Take That' posters all over the walls in the room that had been Janice's' and Joanne's room was covered with posters of the group Steps and Billie Piper.

The girls then entered a large room that stretched to the ceiling of the house. This was clearly the library. Jessica remembered it being bigger. Shelves of books lined the walls from floor to roof. The room was separated by a small balcony. Gold trim metal rails lined the balcony down to the small spiral staircase. Downstairs there was a sliding ladder which could be wheeled around the room to access all the books. Upstairs wasn't as high and only had a two-step ladder to reach the top shelf. Jessica and Charlotte started browsing the book shelves and noticed the usual library selection.

Jessica grabbed Charlottes arm suddenly, "The restricted area."

"Oh, hell yeah," Charlotte replied noticing the gleam in her friends' eye.

"Do you remember where it is from that summer you came across it and my Nan stopped us going in there?" Jessica asked.

Charlotte looked upstairs to the end of the shelf of books at the wooden door that blended in so well a person would miss it if they didn't know it was there. Without a second thought, both the girls charged up the spiral staircase. They were always amazed at how it didn't collapse under their weight, especially with how fragile it looked.

Once the girls reached the door, Jessica slowly opened it. She had never been in the room before so she didn't know what to expect.

Walking into the room she stopped dead in her tracks with a rather disappointed look on her face. "Is this it?"

"What did you expect?" Charlotte asked stopping next to her friend.

"A little more than this," Jessica said motioning around the small room. "I mean seriously, one desk with what looks like an old oil lamp on it, one shelf of books and two arm chairs."

"This room looks as old as the house maybe the books are too?" Charlotte suggested.

"Well going by the dust everywhere I would say nobody came in here very much, if at all," Jessica said looking at the thick layer of dust covering everything.

"I'm going to get a duster, back in a tick," Charlotte said as she walked out of the room.

"Ok," Jessica replied heading for the bookshelf. She noticed that for such a small room it was bright. The tiny square window that the desk sat in front of produced an ample amount of light which encompassed the room quite nicely. She stopped once she reached the bookshelf and noticed the books looked ancient but sturdy. She was rather relieved at that. The last thing she wanted was to pick one up and have it crumble in her hands.

She was so engrossed in checking out the condition of the books that she jumped when Charlotte tapped her on the shoulder.

"So… anything interesting?" Charlotte asked.

"I don't know yet. I haven't started reading book titles," Jessica replied. She read the titles out loud to Charlotte "Alderon, The Last High Fae, The Daughters of Alderon, The Four Prominent Witch Families, Princess Christina of the Fae, Richard King of the Elves, Prince Jordan of the Elves."

"That might have been where your Mum got his name," Charlotte suggested.

"Knock yourself out," Jessica said as she grabbed the polish and duster from her friend. "You have a look, they sound more up your alley than mine."

"Why because one of them mentioned witches?"

"Yep and you own a shop that sells spell books and stuff."

"Fine I will. Make a cuppa when you're done dusting?"

"What did your last slave die of?"

"She hasn't yet," Charlotte said grinning at her friend as she headed towards the books Jessica was just looking at. Grabbing a couple, she sat on one of the arm chairs Jessica had just dusted. She placed the books on her lap and flipped open the top book and started to skim read it. Charlotte skimmed through each book putting it aside when she found nothing of real interest. Half way through the pile she stopped. "That's odd."

"What is?" Jessica asked.

"Well this book isn't finished," Charlotte said while showing Jessica the blank pages. "Look."

"What is that one called?"

"This one would be… Prince Jordan of the Elves. I have to feel sorry for him."

"Why?"

"Well the book starts off with this character named Jordan who falls through a mirror into another realm. He is then kidnapped by his evil uncle for his power. He doesn't even know he has any powers. He gets tortured by his uncle so he can gain his power, he gets rescued…" Charlotte said trailing off in confusion.

"Charlotte what is it?" Jessica asked placing a hand on her friend's arm. Charlotte looked at Jessica.

"Well the book seems to be a fantasy novel especially mentioning elves and other realms. I seem to be getting a Deja vu feeling while reading it, like I dreamt it or something…you know before I started up the dream journal."

"Why would my grandmother have unfinished fantasy novels in a section of the library we were never allowed in?"

Charlotte shrugged and turned her attention back to the book. Her eyes grew wide with shock as she threw the book to the ground as though it had burned her. Jumping up from the chair and knocking the rest of the books from her lap she announced, "Coffee time," and hurried out of the room.

Jessica was shocked by her friend rushing from the room. Shrugging it off, she knelt and slowly picked up the books. She looked towards the shelves and two names caught her attention. Shuffling over to the book shelf she picked up the two books. 'Princess Jessica of the Fae' and 'Charlotte Queen Consort to the Elves' When she read the two book titles she got a shiver run down her spine. Thinking nothing of it she gathered the books and headed for the kitchen.

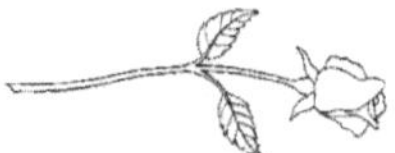

Placing the books on the kitchen table, Jessica looked at her friend. "Charlotte…. what the hell was that?"

"Nothing I just suddenly really needed a coffee." She put Jessica's coffee on the table next to her.

"If you say so," Jessica said not entirely convinced.

"I do, now…. what's this lot you got?" Charlotte said hoping to change the subject.

"I found a couple more books that might be of interest." Jessica opened the books and flipped through the pages. "Or maybe not." she said with a frown.

"Why?"

"They are both blank, look." She handed one of them to Charlotte who started to flip through it. "Why would my Nan have blank books in the restricted area of the library?"

"Maybe they haven't started yet?" Charlotte said shakily.

"What?" Jessica asked in confusion.

"Nothing…. I think we should just finish our exploring before it gets too late."

Jessica looked at her friend and noticed that something had seriously freaked her out when they were in the library.

"Come on then, time to check out Jordan's room I guess." Jessica said not missing the big smile on her friends face as they headed out of the room.

Chapter Six

Jessica felt like a kid sneaking into the living room on Christmas day as she turned the handle to her brother's room. She expected to hear her Grandmother's voice behind her like she had done so many times before, telling her 'Not to even think about it'. Slowly she opened the door waiting for that musty smell of an unused room. When no musty smell touched her nose, she opened the door fully. She flicked on the light switch as she entered the room with an excited Charlotte snapping at her heels.

She noticed her brother's laptop on the bed and stopped so suddenly that Charlotte bumped into her. Jessica stood frozen to the spot. Was he here? She looked behind her and saw that her friend was just as shocked as she was. Glancing around the room, she noticed that it was decorated similar to what his London flat had been. He must have really liked that style she thought as she slowly edged her way towards his bed. She looked over at Charlotte who had gone straight over to the suit cases which sat next to the bed. Jessica could see a glimmer of hope in her friend's eyes.

"Is he here?" Charlotte whispered.

"It looks like he is, but I have a feeling he isn't," Jessica replied. She noticed the room didn't look like it had been unoccupied. "If I didn't know better it would seem as though he had just gone to the loo or something."

Both girls turned their heads to the bathroom and before Jessica could say any more Charlotte bolted around the bed and into the bathroom. The look of disappointment on her friends face when she walked out told her all she needed to know.

"This just doesn't make sense," Jessica said mostly to herself.

"What doesn't?" Charlotte asked as she noticed Jordan's wallet on the bed side table with his car keys. "Look what I just found," she said picking them up and handing them to Jessica.

Jessica grabbed them from her friend and opened the wallet. Money, bank cards, a little bundle of photos. She pulled them out to have a look. Mum, Dad, Janice, Joanne and herself in one photo. Jessica was actually surprised to see one of Charlotte in his wallet and none of Sonya, thank god. Thinking nothing more of it she placed the photos back in his wallet.

Holding the wallet in one hand she tapped it against the other as she thought aloud. "His wallet is here and everything is in it. Car keys are here, so I'm guessing his car must be in the garage." She scanned the room. "No phone, lap top is still plugged in — No way could my Great Uncle have been here for five years and not come in here."

Charlotte giggled. "Not when we've been here for forty-eight hours and have already had a look."

"Ok, I'm going to check his lap top. It will tell us if it has been used recently." She placed the keys and wallet on the bedside table as she sat on the bed in front of her brothers' lap top and switched it on. Jessica glanced at her friend who was now staring out of the bedroom window. "Are you alright?"

"Yeah, just a little confused," Charlotte replied as she started humming the tune to 'I Should Be So Lucky'.

"You and me both," Jessica said shaking her head at her friend.

Focussing back on her brothers' lap top she couldn't help but swear under her breath as the screen requested a password. Not having a clue as to what it could be she decided to randomly type in names. Sonya, Jessica, Joanne, Janice. Nothing. Every name she tried got her nowhere. Suddenly remembering the photo of Charlotte, "I wonder," she whispered looking over at her friend. Typing 'Charlotte' into the box for the password brought the computer to life. That's interesting, she thought cocking her eyebrow.

Jessica couldn't mistake the photo her brother had on his desk top. It was the Christmas before his soul search. He was wearing the jumper that Charlotte had made him. He had a big smile on his face as he stood in the middle of her and Charlotte with Janice and Joanne standing in front of them. Jessica noticed that the picture looked like it had been ripped. She could see that Sonya had been torn out of the original and she guessed that must have been Jordan. Jessica snickered to herself. Her brother had clearly been very unhappy with her not that she could blame him.

Checking over the contents of the computer she found out that her brother hadn't been on it in five years. The last thing he did on his lap top according to the activity logs was start writing down the story's their Nan used to tell them. Her body was consumed with anger as she turned off the laptop and stood from the bed. "Soul searching my arse."

Charlotte jumped at her friend's sudden outburst. "What is it?"

"Jordan hasn't been on his computer in years. His wallet and car keys are here and he is not. My mother knows where my brother is and I'm going to get it out of her if it's the last thing I do." She grabbed his car keys and wallet as she stormed out of the room.

Without thinking Charlotte charged after her. "Jessica!"

"What!" she snapped as she bolted down the stairs.

"You're not going to phone her?"

"No, this is one of those times it would be better in person," she said as she reached the front door.

"How are you going to get there?"

"I'm taking my brothers car," she said as she tossed the keys in the air and caught them. "You coming?"

"I think I'll stay here." Charlotte said. She had seen the dogs scatter when Jessica snapped and didn't think it wise to leave with her friend at the moment.

"I'll be back soon," she said and with that she was gone.

Charlotte shrugged, turned around and headed back up the stairs.

Chapter Seven

Charlotte stood in front of the mirror in Jordan's room. She didn't really know what to do to keep busy while Jessica was at her parents' place. She should have gone with her but Jessica had been so angry before she left even the dogs had steered clear of her so she felt it was better if she stayed behind.

She looked at her reflection in the mirror. She had dressed in her favourite blue jeans with a white t-shirt tucked in and puffed out slightly at the waist. Her black leather heeled shoes added to the eighties look it seemed she was going for. She smiled at her reflection. Her long blonde curls fell over her shoulders from her half up, half down hairstyle and the hair sprayed teased fringe added to the effect. Feeling a little chilly she went to get the jumper that Jessica had given to her the day before. When she returned to the bedroom which contained her belongings she placed her dream journal on the bed side table.

Charlotte then placed her bags on the floor next to Jordan's cases. The reflection of the jumper caught her attention. She headed towards the mirror and noticed the intricate designs weaved into the material, black swirls on a white back ground. Charlotte realised it was the jumper that she had given Jordan one Christmas. She smiled as she remembered the hours she had spent drawing the design on the jumper. The hours that were spent stitching the embroidery which was all in a chain stitch. Had he even worn it? She couldn't recall if she ever saw him in it.

Charlotte smiled as she thought of Jordan even though a tear slowly tracked its way down her cheek. She missed him terribly and could kick herself for still acting like a love-sick teenager. She couldn't help it where he was concerned. The continuous dreams starring him didn't help her any either. She just wished he saw her as more than just his little sisters best friend.

She had never believed Jordan's mothers soul searching story but Charlotte wasn't in a position to argue the point with her. If Jessica didn't argue about it what right had Charlotte to? She suddenly felt overwhelmed, a feeling she had come to know well over the past five years. She decided to lie down for a little while, that usually helped. Walking around to the side of the bed she slowly sat down on the edge and placed her hands in her lap.

"This was a bad idea," she said laying down on her side and grabbing one of the pillows. Strangely enough it still smelt of him so she pulled it tightly to her face and wept into it. Wept for the man she missed and loved with her whole heart and soul. She prayed to see him once again and not only in her dreams.

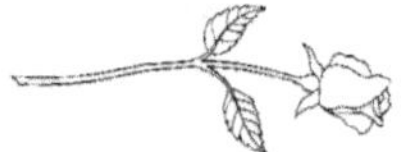

Charlotte woke up with a start and sat up quickly, she hadn't realised she'd fallen asleep. She placed her hand on her heart and tried to slow her breathing. She gradually took in her surroundings and she realised she was still in Jordan's room. She sighed, relieved that she had been dreaming. This dream had been different though and she shuddered as she remembered it. Charlotte grabbed her dream journal and began to write what she could recall, as she had done with all her dreams over the past five years.

I was with Jordan. We were sitting under the old oak tree on a blanket, having a picnic. The sun was shining and Jordan was wearing his blue jeans with a crisp white shirt which was undone. His long hair fell over his shoulders and he was feeding me strawberries. He laughed as one fell onto the long flowing white dress I was wearing. We were happy and having a wonderful afternoon.

Fast Forward to the next part of my dream. I am suddenly in what looks like a cell, my dress is filthy and I'm in pain. I look battered and bruised. Jordan has arrived to come and rescue me from the hell I am in and he grabs my hand. Just as he does someone drags me away from him and I scream his name.

Charlotte stopped writing as she reached the end of what she could remember. She had never kept track of her dreams before but since Jordan had disappeared and was starring in them, she decided to start writing them down. She re-read what she wrote and the part about Jordan having long hair caught her attention.

"That's new," she said out loud. She couldn't recall if she had ever dreamt him having long hair before. It was like he had gone from Johnny Depp in Finding Never Land to Brad Pitt in 'Legends of the Fall.' Although with his hair colour it was more like Tommy Oliver from the Power Rangers.

Smiling to herself she placed her dream journal beside her on the bed and stood up. Grabbing her hair brush from her duffle bag she headed for the mirror. It was still day-light. The sun's rays were pouring into the room from the open curtains. She clearly hadn't slept long and figured that Jessica was still at her parent's place because she hadn't been woken up yet. She dabbed at her eyes which were still red and swollen from all the crying she had recently been doing.

A movement in the mirror pulled her from her thoughts. Were her eyes playing tricks on her? Charlotte was certain she hadn't moved. She froze in fear when she saw another movement in the mirror. Had someone broken into the house? She was too scared to look around from the fear of whom or what she would find.

She realised the movement was from the mirror itself and not a reflection. Curiosity got the better of her and she squinted trying to get a better look at it. Charlotte's eyes widened as her reflection changed before her eyes.

Gradually moving her head back, she realised she was no longer looking at her reflection. She held her breath not knowing what to do. She thought she must be imagining things so she rubbed her eyes and took shallow measured breaths to calm her racing heart. There in the mirror stood a rather handsome man in black. He was staring at her and his long jet black hair was covering half of his face. Chills went down Charlottes back when man grinned at her. It gave her the creepiest feeling.

Before she had time to react the man reached out of the mirror and grabbed Charlotte roughly by the arm and dragged her through it.

Chapter Eight

Jessica knew that it wasn't a good idea to take her brothers Mercedes, especially when she was so full of rage. When the car had actually started it only made it worse. Driving down the motorway she made sure she stuck to the speed limit. She was pissed off, not stupid. Her brother would kill her if she crashed his car.

Pulling up outside her parents' house she got out of the car. She run up the driveway and banged on the front door. A minute later her mother answered it.

"A word. Now." Jessica said as she barged past her mother and headed for the living room.

"Nice to see you too. Isn't that Jordan's car?" Her mother asked as she closed the front door and joined her daughter in the living room.

"Yes, that's Jordan's car. Now where the hell is he?" Jessica said as she held back the urge to yell. The drive hadn't calmed her rage at all.

"I told you, he's soul searching."

"Soul searching my arse. That's crap and you know it. Now where the hell is my brother?" Jessica ignored the urge to stamp her foot like a two-year-old.

"Jessica," Isabella said calmly.

"Don't Jessica me…. Tell me where my brother is, NOW." She couldn't stop from yelling the last word. Her anger had overtaken her common sense.

"What has brought this on?" her mother asked trying not to raise her voice at her daughter's little outburst.

Jessica grabbed the wallet out of her pocket and threw it at her mother.

Isabella caught the wallet and looked at her daughter. "What's this?"

"Jordan's wallet," Jessica said flatly.

"What are you doing with it?"

"A better question would be what Jordan is doing without it... Now where is he and don't give me that soul searching crap. He has been missing for five years and you seem to be the only person who knows about it. You don't seem to care at all where he is or you already know where he is and you won't say anything. What did you do, kill him or something?" Jessica said slowly approaching her mother like a tiger hunting its prey.

"THAT IS ENOUGH!"

Jessica stopped dead in her tracks as her father's voice bellowed through the house. He never yelled. She looked at him with fear and shock on her face. "Sit," he commanded.

Jessica looked behind her and slowly edged her way to the arm chair that was by the fire place. She had not once taken her eyes off her father. Once she was seated, her father cleared his throat.

"Your brother is currently in another realm," he said as calmly as he could. He figured it was pointless to lie.

Jessica laughed sarcastically at her father. She couldn't believe they were trying feed her this story instead of telling her the truth. "You're full of crap."

"Am I?" her father asked raising his eyebrows at her. "And why is that?"

"Because there are no such things as other realms," Jessica said defiantly. "They're just places in the story's Nan used to tell us."

"So, sure. Are you?" Richard asked his daughter. He was thinking about how much fun he was going to have telling her she was going to one.

"Yeah."

"So, I guess your mother and I are lying and we actually killed your brother and buried him under the patio."

"Yes!"

"And why would we have done that?"

"I don't know? I didn't think that far ahead," Jessica said as she lowered her eyes.

"You didn't think at all," he said, slightly raising his voice.

Jessica's tears welled up in her eyes. Her dad always had that effect on her when he raised his voice, even just slightly. She looked up at her father and couldn't believe her eyes as she watched his slowly turn silver.

Richard looked over at his wife. "Something is wrong"

Isabella looked at her husband and her daughter. She smiled at the shocked look on her daughter's face. She would love to hear Jessica's explanation for her father's current eye colour.

"Has the Call of the Rose started?" she asked. Richard shook his head.

"Go and call Trixie."

"What's the Call of the Rose?" Jessica asked.

"Not really the time to explain that," Richard said, looking at his daughter.

"Ok…. So, who's Trixie?" Jessica asked still mesmerised by her dad's eyes.

"My little sister," he told her.

"You have a sister?" Jessica couldn't stop the sound of shock in her voice. Had she even met this sister?

"I have a brother too," Richard said. His daughter's anger turned to surprise and then to shock. "For someone who does genealogy professionally, you know very little about your own family."

"Why have we never met them?" Jessica asked. She was ashamed that there was some truth to her father's words.

"Jordan has," he said flatly. "You probably wouldn't remember meeting my sister."

"Where do they live?"

"In another realm. Well, the Elvin Realm to be exact. Not the one that you're going too." Richard said. He thought he should just throw that in there to save him trying to tell her later.

"Not that other realm crap again-wait-what?" Jessica said looking blankly at her father.

"Oh yes. You're to go to the one your Nan currently resides in."

"WHAT." Jessica bolted off the chair. "I'm gonna die?"

"What?" said Richard totally confused.

"Um…Darling," Isabella said getting her husband's attention. "The girls don't know, remember."

"Don't know what?" Jessica asked looking at her mother.

"I may as well tell you because you're going to find out soon enough any way. My mother didn't actually die, nor did my Dad. They went back to the realms they are from."

"Realms they are from?" Jessica said raising an eye brow at her mother.

"Yes…. All those stories my Mum used to tell you when you were little, happen to be true. Well, most of them anyway." Isabella shrugged. "I would say that we could get Jordan to confirm it for you but he would be busy getting things ready for your arrival."

"My arrival."

"Yes, you're …."

Both the women turned to look at Richard, who was way too quiet. Jessica wondered why her dad was standing in front of the mirror. His hand was on the glass and his eyes were closed. He looked as though he was having a conversation with someone but she could only see her father and couldn't hear anyone else.

Jessica froze with fear at the look on her father's face as he turned around. Dread filled the pit of her stomach.

"Who was at Rose Manor?" he asked, his voice was void of emotion.

"What do you mean was?"

"Exactly what I said. So, who was there?"

"Charlotte was," Jessica said in a panic as she bolted for the door.

"Jessica wait," Richard yelled after his daughter but his words had fallen on deaf ears.

Chapter Nine

Jordan stood in the grand ball room of the Palace of the Fae. He had been overjoyed when his Grandmother said he could organise it for his sister's arrival into the Realm. As the Prince of the Elves it wasn't his job to get things ready for her but his Grandmother had known how much he missed his sisters so allowed him to take over with the preparations. He was only to come to her if he needed to.

Looking at the long 'to-do' list he had prepared with his grandmothers help, he was suddenly brought to his knees as a surge of emotions hit him all at once. "What the hell" he said aloud. His long hair that covered his face hid the fact that he was somehow overwhelmed with fear. He slowly began to stand and he was breathing hard as he waited to see if his legs would give out from under him. Once he was on his feet he braced himself against the long table and tried to control his breathing to diminish the fear he felt.

Closing his eyes, he sensed that someone was in fear someone he knew. It wasn't one of his sisters, he would have felt that. But he did know this person and had a strong connection to them but he couldn't place who it was. One of his personal guards entered interrupting his thoughts. He looked at the guard who was knelt in front of him with his head bowed. "You have news?" Jordan asked him.

"Yes, your highness," the guard said raising his head to look at Jordan. "A woman has been brought through from the human realm."

"What do you mean a woman has been brought from the human realm?" Jordan asked.

"We believe Vincent has stolen her from the human realm. We do not know the identity of the young woman. We think Vincent was attempting to take your sister."

"You think?" Jordan braced himself again and grabbed the edge of the table so tightly his knuckles went white. Not only did the mention of Vincent leave a vile taste in his mouth but he had now attempted to kidnap one of his sisters. *'What was that bloke's problem?'* Jordan thought to himself.

"Yes, your highness. As we all know your sister is due to arrive soon so we assumed he was meant to take her but got the wrong person. Vincent was seen hastily leaving the Manor House of the neutral realm with a young blonde woman and—"

"Blonde!" Jordan said interrupting his guard.

"Yes, your highness," the guard said looking up at his Prince.

"Didn't anyone think to stop him?" Jordan asked.

"Vincent used his power to subdue us, we couldn't move until he had flashed out of the realm."

Jordan was gradually filling with rage at the audacity of his Uncle's actions. He was being flooded by a multitude of emotions all at once, he needed to regain control. He needed to think and couldn't do that with an audience.

"That will be all," Jordan said, formally dismissing his guard. "And, thank you," he said as an afterthought. Jordan watched as his guard stood and with a nod of his head he turned and was gone.

Jordan stood there as the thoughts rushed through his mind. Why the fact the girl had been blonde caught his attention, he didn't know. He knew which sister was due to arrive and suddenly the realisation of who it could be made his heart drop to his stomach like stone.

"Charlotte," he whispered, not noticing the tear streaking down his check. *'It can't be her,'* he thought slamming his fist on the table in frustration. What the hell was happening to him, his emotions were all over the place.

"Hey sweet pea, what's up?" said a cheery voice.

Turning his head to see who it was he replied. "Hey Trixie!"

Trixie walked over to her nephew and placed her hand on his shoulder "What's up?" she asked tenderly, noticing the tear on his check.

"It would seem that your brother has taken Jessica's best friend Charlotte from the human realm." Jordan answered through gritted teeth. He was trying not to convey any emotion in his voice but was failing in the attempt.

"Ooh the pretty blonde. Yeah I heard about that."

"No keeping anything from you, hey." Jordan said sharply.

"Nope," Trixie said rubbing her hands together. "So, Vincent strikes back."

"Seriously?" Jordan said looking totally dumbfounded. "You're quoting Star Wars?"

Trixie looked at him innocently. "What! Would you have preferred me say, revenge of the uncle?"

Jordan just stared at his Aunt in total disbelief. "How can you make jokes at a time like this? You really can be an insensitive bitch sometimes."

Trixie smiled at him knowing something he didn't.

"What are you smiling at?" he asked her with a disgusted look.

"Nothing…. So, what makes you think it was this Charlotte that was taken?" she asked him. She was curious to hear what the answer would be.

"Jessica is due to arrive soon and would have been drawn to the house as I was. Charlotte has never been far from Jessica as they have been inseparable since childhood and she, no doubt, would have gone with her."

"That doesn't mean it was Charlotte." Trixie pointed out. "Maybe Jessica hadn't gone to the house yet."

"That is possible. However, Charlotte is the only blonde friend any of my sisters have."

"You haven't been there in five years. Maybe it's a friend you haven't met."

Jordan shook his head. "No, it has to be Charlotte."

"Why does it have to be her and not someone else?"

"Because I felt like I knew the person and I had a surge of emotions shoot through me. What the hell is that all about?"

Confirmation one, Trixie thought to herself. She turned her nephew so he faced her. "Look at me," she said and Jordan slowly lifted his head to look at his aunt. "If it is in fact her, you will find her no matter where Vincent takes her."

"How can you be so sure?" he said feeling defeated and not understanding why.

"Because, you are the only one who can."

"What is that supposed to mean?"

"Let's go and have a little chat to your mother. Some things are better left for parents to explain," Trixie said while dragging her confused looking nephew out of the ball room.

Chapter Ten

When she arrived back at the house Jessica flung open the front door. It opened so fast and hard that it hit the wall it was connected to and nearly smashed. She didn't notice that the green rose bud now had a black tendril creeping along the stem slowly making its way up the petals of the bud, her only thought was for her friend. The look on her father's face earlier put the fear of god in her concerning the safety of her friend. Jessica knew her parents would be there shortly. She had driven past them on the motorway more than once. In her haste to get back she lane jumped and kept getting caught behind traffic as her parents drove casually by.

She bolted up the stairs towards her brother's bedroom leaving the door open.

"Charlotte," she bellowed.

Bursting through the door she came to a halt, noticing the room was empty. After running through the house searching for her Jessica returned to Jordan's room. Maybe she had just popped down the shops and Jessica was just over reacting? She noticed that Charlotte had left her dream journal in the middle of the bed and she walked over and picked it up. Jessica turned to the last page and read the entry. A feeling of dread made its way into the pit of her stomach. Charlotte had dreamt she had been taken. Jessica wondered what else Charlotte had dreamt about. She sat on the bed with one leg dangling over the side, flicking through the pages and skim reading the contents. Jessica read allowed the entry's that caught her attention.

Jordan introduced me to his Aunt today. Trixie her name was, she said she was an Elf. I remembered giggling at her because she looked more like a Pixie. I also saw Jordan's Nan again. I remembered wishing that Jessica was sharing my dream so she could see her Nan as well. She told me she was a Princess in the land of the Fae. Jordan took me there and it was beautiful. It was much nicer than the elfin realm that Jordan oversaw while his Dad was away. He was about to tell me something very important when I woke up.

Most of the entries were similar and Charlotte was always with Jordan. It read more like a diary, as though Charlotte had actually lived it rather than dreamt it. Her dad had said his sister's name was Trixie. Charlotte couldn't possibly have known that and the fact that her Grandmother was still alive. Her friend either had one hell of an imagination or Jessica had seriously been thrown into the twilight zone.

Jessica saw something out of the corner of her eye so she looked up. The mirror had caught her attention. Putting her friend's journal back down on the bed she stood up slowly. She walked towards the mirror and felt a sudden pain in her foot. She lifted her foot and looked down to see what she had trodden on. Charlotte's hair brush was just lying on the floor. Jessica bent down to pick it up but movement in the mirror stopped her in her tracks. Jessica looked between her legs to see if someone had come in. A sudden feeling of fear engrossed her when she realised that nobody was there. She lifted her head slowly to look at the mirror once again knowing what she saw was coming from there. She startled upright in shock at who she was looking at.

"What the hell?" she said just before she feinted.

"Ah crap," Jordan said as he stepped through the mirror.

Chapter Eleven

Jessica opened her eyes and found her mother sitting on Jordan's bed beside her. Her Dad was standing by the window which made it look so small.

"What happened?" she asked trying to sit up.

"You feinted," her mother replied.

"Why did you put me in Jordan's bed?"

"We didn't," Isabella said feeling sorry for her son suddenly. Thank god, she'd mentioned to him that his sisters hadn't been told where he had been.

"Who the hell did?"

"I did," said a voice from the shadows.

Jessica knew that voice. She looked around her mother and her eyes widened in shock as her brother stepped out of the shadows. Jessica took a good look at him. He was wearing blue jeans and white t-shirt. The usual stuff her brother wore. His long hair fell past his shoulders but however did not look the same as it had during his heavy metal phase. Thoughts of Charlottes dream journal suddenly popped into her mind as she remembered he had long hair in her last entry. She rubbed her eyes to make sure she wasn't dreaming. She looked back and forth between her mother and brother in total disbelief.

"I'm here," Jordan said as he stepped forward. Then he watched as realisation dawned on his sisters' face. Then he watched as that look of disbelief changed to rage. "Ah shit," he said as he braced himself for the storm that was his little sister.

Jessica glared at her brother slowly pulling the covers from her legs. If looks could kill he would have died a thousand deaths. She slowly approached her brother like a predator ready to attack its prey.

Suddenly she lost control of her emotions and burst into tears. She thumped her brother's chest over and over again, letting out the frustration she felt from five years of worrying about him and the unknown.

Jordan stood there not moving for the first few thumps and letting his sister get it out of her system. He had always been closer to Jessica than his other two sisters and if this is what he got from her, the other two would be like a walk in the park. Slowly putting his arms around his sister, he pulled her into a tight embrace kissing the top of her head.

"I'm here now," he said as he stroked her hair and rubbed slow circles down her back to calm her. He didn't know what was worse. Her punching him out of anger which hurt like hell because she knew how to punch. Or the heart wrenching sobs that were racking her body as she cried in his arms. Pulling his sister tighter to him he decided he preferred to be punched. Her uncontrollable sobs were tearing at his heart. Releasing his hold on her he held her out so he could see her face. "Better now?" he asked as he wiped the tears from her eyes.

"Git," she said as she jokingly slapped his arm. Smiling at her big brother she flicked his long hair over his shoulders. "What's with the Brad Pitt look?" she continued as if they had never been apart.

"Something different," Jordan replied on a shrug.

"Fair enough then," she said as they made their way towards their parents.

"Ok, what's the deal here?" Jessica said looking from her parents to her brother and back again.

"First things first," Richard said as he looked at his son. "How is Trixie?"

"The usual. Quoting Star Wars at every opportunity," Jordan replied flatly.

"Why does that not surprise me? Why didn't she come here with you?"

"She said something about doing recon, but wouldn't go into details."

"Bloody sisters," he said while shaking his head. He looked at his two older children. He had a lot of explaining to do especially where

Jessica was concerned. Now seemed like as good a time as any. He looked over at his wife. "Would you be so kind as to make some tea?"

"And where are you going, may I ask?" enquired Isabella. She recognised her husband's tone of voice.

"To get the family box from the attic."

"A wooden one, with no lock on it?" asked Jessica suddenly.

"Have you and Charlotte been in the attic?" Isabella asked.

"Yeah, we were exploring the house…was that a bad thing?" Jessica asked. Suddenly feeling like a ten-year-old about to get grounded for being naughty.

"No," her father said. "That will make things a little easier. Shall we," he said motioning to the bedroom door.

Chapter Twelve

As he walked into the kitchen Richard noticed all the items the girls had placed on the table. "You and Charlotte have been busy in the library as well, I see?" he said stopping in front of the large box from the attic. He waved his hand in front of the box and it opened.

"How the hell did you do that?" Jessica asked standing opposite her brother at the table.

"Magic!" he said smiling at her.

"Not that again," Jessica said rolling her eyes.

Jordan looked at his sister then his father. "Shouldn't we be getting Charlotte back?"

Jessica stared at her brother. All hopes that Charlotte had gone out shopping were dashed with that one question. "Back? Where the hell is she that we need to get her back? Back from where?"

"Patience."

Jordan and Jessica stared at their father in shock.

"We will get Charlotte back. However, it would come in handy if we made sure it is definitely her that has been taken."

"I know it's her. This is wasting time we could be using to get her back," Jordan said with frustration and motioning to the items on the table.

Richard looked at his son. "How do you know it's her and where do you suggest we start?"

"I felt her as she came into the realm. I was also over whelmed with fear, it brought me to my knees and —"

"Where were you when this happened?" Richard asked cutting his son off.

"I was in the Fae castle getting things ready for when Jessica arrived."

Richard started looking through the box in front of him. He found what he was looking for and he unrolled the parchment. Confirming his thoughts, he handed the parchment to his wife.

Isabella looked at the parchment but didn't need the confirmation of something she already knew. "Darling, we have known this for years," she stated handing it back to him.

"We have?"

"Well I have, but I tend to notice more than you do," Isabella said walking over to the kettle to finish making the drinks.

"You do know that Vincent has her right?" Jordan asked his father. He was getting frustrated with everyone's lack of action. "You remember what he did to me?"

Richard looked at his son. "If I know my brother, he will not hurt her unless provoked." Richard said not quite knowing how to put the next part. "He will more than likely try and seduce her instead."

"WHAT!" Jordan and Jessica yelled in unison. They both flew off their chairs almost knocking them flying.

"Sit down." Isabella said firmly as she carried a tray full of mugs to the table. Jordan took the tray from his mother and placed it on the table as they all took their seats.

"Why would Vincent attempt to seduce Charlotte? I mean, what could he possibly have to gain by it?" Jordan asked with uncertainty in his voice.

"The satisfaction of her willingly giving herself to him, knowing that she is not his to have," Richard said looking at his son.

"What do you mean not his to have?" Jordan asked rather surprised at the tone of his voice.

Isabella placed a hand on her son's arm not at all surprised that he had asked the questions and not Jessica. "Do you believe in soul mates?"

"Yes." What was it with people asking him that question Jordan wondered?

"Well, Charlotte has one and Vincent knows who he is."

"Who is it?" Jordan asked not understanding why he feared the answer.

"All in good time," his father said as he took a seat. Looking at his daughter he added. "You have rather expensive tastes."

"What?" she asked in confusion. "What makes you say that?"

"The house is magical and changes to meet the taste of the occupier. Marble is everywhere."

"Ok let's forget the first bit of what you said for a minute and focus on the second bit. Are you saying that it's real marble?"

"Yep, possibly from ancient Greece itself."

"How?" Jessica asked even more confused, thinking her dad was going mental.

"I told you, magic," he said. The look that he gave her made her slump back in her chair with a scowl on her face.

Jessica casually picked up one of the books she had flipped through earlier. She opened it to the front page and froze trying to comprehend what she was seeing. There was no writing in the book earlier. Without reading what was now written in the book she turned it over to see which one she had picked up, 'Charlotte Queen Consort of the Elves'. She slowly placed the book on the table and looked at her brother who appeared to be deep in thought. *'I wonder,'* she thought to herself as she looked for the book titled, 'Jordan Prince of the Elves.'

"What are you doing?" whispered her mother.

"I'm testing out a theory," Jessica replied. She found the book she had been searching for and flipped to the last page with writing on it. She stared at the page and found it was writing itself. This must have been what happened when Charlotte was looking at it before when she freaked out. Skimming over the page it dawned on her the book was writing events as they happened. She handed the book to her mother before addressing her brother. "So, Jordan. Did you actually fall through the mirror in your room?"

Jordan just stared at her and she smiled at him. "Charlotte thought you were an idiot for that." If looks could kill she thought when she saw the look on her brother's face.

"Jessica."

"Yes Daddy," she said in her most innocent little girl voice.

"You will find the book also says your brother was tortured. Now stop winding him up and have a look at this." Richard passed her the old piece of parchment that contained the family tree. He needed something to distract her from tormenting her brother. He shook his head subconsciously at the pair of them, it was though they were little kids again.

Jessica looked at the family tree her father had given her. Elves, Witches and Fae were written all over it. Christina of the Fae, Tristan of the Harmonious Witches, Richard King of the Elves. Following the names down, she found Jordan's name. She looked at her father in disbelief, "This is our tree?" He nodded. "So, you're actually an elf?" He nodded again. Jessica looked at her brother. "Did you know this?"

"Yes, I've actually seen Dad in his elf form…. Hang on what book?" Jordan asked looking at his father.

"This one," Jessica said. She picked up the book from where their mother had put it and handed it to him.

Jordan skimmed through the book, cringing at the memories. "You knew there was a book which is basically documenting my life?" Jordan asked looking at his father.

"I knew there were books like that."

"And you didn't think to mention it, or read it to find me quicker when I was captured. This tells you exactly where I was being kept."

"I didn't know there was a book on you and as I recall it was you who decided to go to the house when your mother asked you not too. Plus, it has been so long since those books have surfaced. I had completely forgotten they even existed. The last time I laid eyes on them they were scrolls in a jar."

"Seriously," Jessica said looking at her father.

"Yes," he said flatly.

"So how old would that make you?" Jessica asked not hiding the cheekiness in her voice.

Richard looked at his daughter with amusement. "A lot older than I look."

"So how old does that make Mum?"

"Not that old thank you very much," Isabella replied slightly insulted.

"Your mother is the age she is meant to be, even if she does not look it," Richard replied while smiling fondly at his wife and giving her a wink.

"The tree doesn't actually give any dates," Jessica said as she stood and walked over to her father taking the family tree with her. "And what does this mean?" she said as she pointed to a section of the tree.

"You're a genealogist, you tell me."

Jessica looked over the words again.

'Jordan Jason Elfin chosen to Charlotte Sapphire Louise Finnissy-Soul Mate Found'

"I'm guessing it is indicating that those two are soul mates. But why have I got question marks next to my name?" Jessica asked her father.

"You have yet to meet your soul mate. If you notice Janice found hers."

"Good job she fell pregnant to him then hey."

"That's not funny Jessica," Richard said scowling at his daughter. "The fact that Scott was indeed her soul mate stopped me from ripping his bloody head off." His daughter falling pregnant so soon after her eighteenth birthday was still a very sore spot where he was concerned. He loved both his grand-daughters dearly and Janice was very happy but it still rubbed him up the wrong way how it all happened.

Jessica looked at the tree once more.

Janice Isabella Elfin Joined with Scott Michael Mitchell

Children - Alysha Marie Mitchell, Emily Claire Mitchell, ???, ???

"Why are there two lots of question marks after the girl's names?" Jessica asked.

"There are possibly two more children yet to be born," Richard replied. "As you may have noticed the question marks are also faded. This means that those two children may not be born at all."

Richard pointed to her name on the tree. "You're to have three children and Jordan is to have five. However, they are even more faded since you are not with anyone. The tree would no doubt change again if you ended up with someone other than your soul mate. You might have ten kids instead." Richard grinned at the horrified look on his daughter's face.

"Okay, so why has it got chosen to for Jordan and you know," she said nodding her head in her brother's direction. "And nothing else?" Jessica was hoping to change the subject of her having children.

Isabella decided to jump in. "Because they are not married, for want of a better explanation. Everyone still has free will and they may not end up together at the end of it. Granted we know the feelings are there on both sides," she said glancing at Jordan who was reading through the book about himself. "Even if one of them doesn't realise it yet."

Chapter Thirteen

Getting frustrated Jordan threw the book across the room. Everyone stopped what they were doing to look at him.

"Is something the matter?" Richard asked his son, raising an eyebrow.

"Everything is just dandy," Jordan replied sarcastically as he started to mindlessly flick through the other books, not actually reading what they said.

Isabella went over to retrieve the book from its resting place on the floor and looked at her son. Opening the book to the last page she silently began to read. She knew this would tell her exactly what was on her son's mind even if he wouldn't.

'Jordan sat in the kitchen of the human realm. Frustration was building inside him like a volcano about to erupt. He couldn't believe the lack of action to get Charlotte back. He was a hands-on kind of guy. Sitting here going through old documents to him, was a waste of time. Time, he could be using to search for her. He didn't know why he felt so strongly about it. His sister, who was Charlotte's best friend seemed totally at ease.'

Isabella looked at her daughter and then back to her son. His face conveyed everything that she was currently reading. The glazed look he had in his eyes told her he was reminiscing about something. She dragged her attention back to the book and she continued to read.

'He remembered the first time he had met Charlotte. She was five and his little sister's new friend at school. The second she saw him Charlotte grabbed a book out of her bag and climbed up onto his lap and handed him the book. All she said was "story" while she wiggled her bum to get herself comfy.

'Other memories of Charlotte rushed through his mind like a video on fast forward. Anger pulsed through him when he remembered Jessica and Charlotte's school ball

and the events of that night. He remembered having a heart broken Charlotte in his arms and a pissed off Jessica who wanted to rip some blokes head off. Some of the memories he had long forgotten about were now flashing through his mind. Even the dreams he had of Charlotte while he was in the Realm of the Elves. The ones that had seemed so real he....'

Isabella looked up as the book stopped writing. She noticed Jordan was sitting and watching her. *'That explains why it stopped writing'* she thought to herself as she closed the book and put it down.

"Interesting, was it?" Jordan asked her sarcastically.

"Very enlightening," she replied smiling at him. She knew emotionally he was all over the place. The fact he didn't understand why, made it worse. He would be no good to Charlotte in this state, it was time to make him realise why.

"Jordan sweetie, what book was it?"

"What?" he said to his mother in confusion.

"The book Charlotte got you to read to her when you were what? Nine?" Isabella asked nonchalantly, she knew he hadn't been nine at the time.

"I was ten and it was 'The Tiger Who Came to Tea' why?"

"Do you remember what you were doing before you picked the girls up from their school ball?"

Jordan sat there racking his brain for the memory. He didn't notice that his father and sister had now sat down to listen to his mother's brand of a Spanish inquisition. "No and I will ask again, why?"

"Just humour me and try to remember."

"I got nothing," he said frustrated with his mother and her questions.

"You my darling son were in the middle of a romantic dinner with Sonya at my place. I can't remember why? When your phone went off to the ring tone of…. oh, what was it again? Oh yes, I remember now. 'Everything I do, I do it for you.' You raced to the phone so fast you sent the chair flying."

"So," Jordan shrugged as the memories of that night came flooding back to him.

"After answering the phone, you grabbed your car keys and headed towards the front door. When Sonya asked you what was going on all you said was you needed go. I take it Sonya knew that was the ring tone you had for Charlotte?"

"She did."

"Why did you have that ring tone for Charlotte?" Isabella asked him. She was a little confused as to why but figured subconsciously he had chosen it because of the first verse of the song.

"I don't know. Wasn't it her favourite film at the time?"

"No," said Jessica.

"Oh." That was all Jordan could say. *Why did he have that as a ring tone for Charlotte,'* he thought to himself before turning back to his mother so she could continue.

"I thought she did. You couldn't miss the anger on her face when your phone went off or the fact that she was very pissed off when she told you that if you walked out the door your relationship was over. What did you say and do before you walked out the door?" Isabella asked her son, remembering the night very well.

"I shrugged and said whatever." That he remembered like it was yesterday. Changing the subject, he asked. "How is the two-timing bitch?" he spat.

"Well, she has a son now. He is nearly four. Such a little darling he is."

"Who's the father? Does she even know?" Jordan couldn't help the snide comment flying out of his mouth.

"She claimed the father was Michael. He denied it of course claiming that she cheated on him."

"And you don't believe him?" Jordan asked raising his eyebrow at the look on his mother's face.

"It's not that I don't believe him exactly. It's just that her son is the spitting image of someone who couldn't possibly be the father."

"Who?"

"Well he is the spitting image of your father's brother."

"Isabella, not that again. There is no way that Vincent is that child's father," Richard said scolding his wife.

Jordan looked at his parents he could clearly tell this was an argument they must have had many times.

"He could be," Jordan said flatly. "He did fuck her after all."

"When?" Richard and Isabella asked as one.

"In the Elvin Realm," Jordan replied. "Before he chained me up."

"So, he would be the father," Isabella said triumphantly.

"Isabella the timing is wrong. We know for a fact that she has been just up the road from us for the last five years."

"What, he couldn't have been in the human realm with her?" Jordan inquired.

"Not without me knowing it."

"But you did know he was here, you said you could sense him," Isabella said.

"He was miles away, possibly in Australia or America," Richard exclaimed raising his arms for emphasis.

"Was he?" Isabella questioned, folding her arms over her chest.

"Of course, he was. I would have sensed it, had he been closer."

"Not if he had used a hiding potion."

"The price for those potions is power and a lot of it. Besides neither Tristan nor Ruby would not have made him such a thing."

"My father and Ruby are not the only witches he knows," Isabella bellowed at him. "Plus, he was overdosing on power when he took Jordan's and you didn't get the chance to take all of it back."

Jordan looked at his parents in stunned silence. It was rare that they argued and even rarer that they argued in front of him or his sisters. His father stood there in silence, looking as if he was trying to work out something in his head. His mother was sitting and breathing heavily. She was clearly fuming. Jessica was just sitting there looking over the family tree completely oblivious to anything.

"Give me that," Richard snapped as he grabbed the scroll containing the tree out of his daughter's hand.

"Oi!" Jessica snapped back, throwing a filthy look at her father.

"Well I'll be damned." Richard said as he looked at the family tree. His breath caught as he noticed three lots of faded question marks and the name 'Jayden' next to Joanne's name. He was sure that hadn't been there an hour ago, he looked at Isabella and whispered, "I'll be double damned."

"So, what were we talking about?" Isabella said as she watched her husband sit in the chair with a stunned look on his face.

"School ball and Sonya," Jessica replied, trying to be helpful.

Jordan threw his sister a dirty look hoping to stay off that subject.

"I don't get why she would cheat on me in the first place? Never mind continued to do so for years." Jordan still felt like a fool for being blind to the fact.

"I guess she got fed up with competing with Charlotte for your affections," Isabella murmured.

"That's basically what she said, but that's crap and you know it," Jordan snapped pointing at his mother.

"Really! On the night of the school ball you effectively ended your relationship when you left the house to be a 'knight in shining armour' to a damsel clearly in distress. Granted, you were back together a week or two later, but that particular night where did you spend it?"

"If I recall correctly, I spent the night on your settee as I did for the whole two weeks."

"But that night, were you all alone on my settee?" Isabella asked. She was deliberately getting her son worked up. He clearly didn't want to talk about it.

Jordan gave his mother a filthy look. "You know damn well I wasn't alone."

"Jessica darling," Isabella asked looking at her daughter "Do you remember where Charlotte slept that night?"

"Yeah, she was on the settee with Jordan. You put a foot stool under his feet because he looked uncomfortable sleeping sitting up. Then you put a blanket over them," Jessica replied looking at her mother then her brother. "I didn't even know Charlotte had called Jordan until he turned up. That could be because I was more concerned with wanting to smack someone's face in. Good job he turned up, otherwise I would have."

"So, I fell asleep with her hugged up to me. She was upset, what was I meant to do?"

"Let Jessica handle it." Isabella stated.

"Well I couldn't do that," Jordan said through clenched teeth.

"And why not? What made you be the one to comfort her?"

"Because it broke my heart to hear her so upset on the phone," Jordan suddenly snapped in anger. He stood up and continued his rant.

"Do you seriously think I gave a rat's arse about Sonya or what she thought? In that moment, she could have gone to hell for all I cared."

"And what if Sonya had tried to stop you going out the door?" Isabella asked, not phased at all by her son's actions.

"She wouldn't have dared," Jordan said. His voice had taken on a deadly tone.

"Why?" Isabella couldn't help but ask. She had gotten her son worked up and was rather surprised at how easy it had been. Granted the conversation about Vincent probably didn't help her son's emotional state. Clearly Charlotte was a weakness of his and with luck he was about to realise it.

"Because I would have shoved her out of the way."

"Why?" It was Jessica who asked this time, confused at her brother's admission.

"Because there is nothing and nobody that would stop me from getting to the woman I love."

Jordan sat down stunned. He felt like he'd been hit with a sledge hammer as all his emotions crashed into him at once. His words were only now starting to sink in. He was in love with Charlotte and unbeknownst to him, always had been.

"That took you long enough," Isabella said triumphantly.

Chapter Fourteen

Charlotte couldn't help her skin crawling every time the man in black looked at her. She didn't know where she was, how she got there or who he was. His features were hidden in darkness. The small amount of light that shone through a tiny window allowed her to at least see where he was.

She had been chained to what looked like cement blocks. The shackles around her wrists were on long chains which allowed a little movement in her arms. She could stand without any problems but she was still restricted. She hadn't been able to move at all until he chained her up. It was like he was using magic to keep her still and had been since he dragged her through Jordan's mirror. She didn't know how any of this was even possible. She did know that she wished more than anything that Jordan was there to be her knight once again.

Charlotte froze as the man in black started moving towards her, bringing her out of her little fantasy. He was looking her up and down and continued to do so as he slowly walked around her. She couldn't believe he was actually checking her out. Why was he behaving like this? Deciding what to do with his latest purchase? Her stomach rolled at the thoughts of what he had planned.

The man came to a stop in front of her and since he was no longer shrouded in darkness she could get a better look at her captor. Charlotte thought he was quite handsome while his lustful silver eyes roamed all over her. *Wait— what— silver eyes, how the hell?'* She was roused from her thoughts as his hand reached to touch her face. She closed her eyes when she felt what seemed like a long finger nail touch her check. She could feel the nail trace down her jaw line, down her heck and along her shoulder. Charlotte closed her eyes tight against the sensation and the feeling of dread that was welling up inside of her.

"You are a pretty one that's for sure, it's no wonder I desire you." The man spoke in a low and sultry voice which conveyed the desire in his eyes.

Charlotte quickly opened her eyes and came face to face with a grin that gave her the creeps. Trying to forget about the fear churning inside her and throwing caution to the wind she decided to find out what she could. She looked at his silver eyes and got lost for a moment. Under different circumstances those eyes could make any girl melt with desire but at the moment they just gave her the creeps. She decided to ask him straight "Who are you and what do you want with me?"

The man in black took his hand from her shoulder and stepped back, bowing at the waist. "I am Vincent." he said taking a step towards her he was so close his face was only inches from hers. "And I want you."

Fear churned inside her stomach and made its way to the surface. "Why me?" she asked trying to disguise the fear in her voice.

"Simple," he said taking a step back. "You are not mine to have, which is why I want you."

"What are you going to do? Force yourself on me?" She felt sick just thinking about it.

Vincent took a step towards her and grabbed one of her chained hands and brought it to his lips, holding it there. "I may be evil my dear, but I'm not a monster," he said as he glanced up to make eye contact with her. "Why force, when I can seduce," he said smugly and placed a kiss on her hand which made her shudder.

"Seduce?" she said, her voice wavering. *This is so not how I want to lose my virginity or the man I want seducing me'* she thought just as Vincent spoke again.

"Yes, my dear. What would be the point of me forcing myself on you, as you put it? I care not for the self-gratification part of things. Nor do I care for the feeling of being in control. That is not the type of power I crave. Seducing you would be much more beneficial."

"So why seduce me?" Charlotte asked. She wondered what made her so special that he would go to such lengths to get her into bed. She figured that with his looks he would have no problems filling his bed.

"Because it would be much more gratifying for me to see the hurt and pain on my nephews' face when he found out that the woman he was destined to be with chose willingly to come to my bed. It would be even better if he was to witness it."

"I think you have me confused with someone else," Charlotte said. This guy was obviously having a laugh.

"And why is that?" he asked. He was rather intrigued as to what she would say next.

"Cause. I'm not with anybody. I very much doubt that I am meant to be with anyone. Especially your nephew, whoever the hell that is. So, if you would be so kind as to let me go, you can get back to searching for the person you are actually looking for."

Vincent raised an eyebrow at her in amusement. "True you are not the original person I was going for, but having you here works out much better than my niece would have."

"And who is your niece?"

"Why…Jessica."

"Jessica? As in Jessica Elfin, my best friend Jessica?" said Charlotte shocked.

"I think the answer could possibly be yes to that question."

"So why did you take me, if you were after Jessica?" she asked as she placed her hands on her hips. The fact that Jordan would be his nephew or why taking her was better than having Jessica didn't even register.

"You were there," he said shrugging nonchalantly.

"That's it, because I was there!!" Anger surged through her at the thought. "Not a very good plan was it."

"I don't know. The little hiccup in my plan has worked out better than I would have imagined," he said smirking at her.

"What are you smirking at?" she asked still slightly annoyed that he hadn't unchained her.

Vincent knew that she was Jordan's soul mate but what if she didn't have an emotional attachment to him yet? Jordan had been away from the human realm for five years and that could have made a difference. He needed to know, especially if his plan was to work.

"I wonder what Jordan would have to say about you being kidnapped and chained up like this?" Vincent asked. He watched her face closely for any indication that she felt something for him.

"I imagine he would be pissed off," Charlotte replied.

"Why would he be pissed off? It's not like you know him."

"I've known him since I was five years old thank you very much," Charlotte said angrily.

"So, he would probably think of you like another little sister." Vincent knew how the soul mate bonds worked. He still remembered how it felt to have a soul mate. Even after almost a century since her passing.

"Probably," Charlotte said with a shrug.

The look on Charlotte's face told him all he needed to know. She was very much in love with Jordan and had been for years. This, he could use to his advantage. Even if Jordan hadn't noticed any romantic feelings for this girl, she had them for him. Even though she was trying to hide them.

"Seducing you is going to be a welcomed challenge."

"Why would you say that?" Charlotte asked a little confused.

Vincent took a step towards her. Standing only inches from her he raised his hand and gently ran the back of his fingers down her check. He lowered his head so his lips were only inches away from her ear. "You really have no idea who you are meant to be with, do you?"

"I told you I'm not meant to be with anyone. I'm going to die a lonely old woman with many cats."

"You will if I get my way with you," Vincent replied lifting his head. He grinned when he saw the anger on her face. She was a feisty one, he liked that.

"And what would make you say that?"

"Because my dear, the young man that you are in fact meant to be with couldn't possibly bring himself to want you after I have been with you."

"Why would you say that? Did you do something to him?" she asked thinking there was a reason for the wording he used.

"I tortured him and enjoyed every minute of it," Vincent replied smiling. Charlotte didn't like the evil gleam he had in his eyes.

Charlotte glared at him. "You unfeeling, selfish mother f —"

Vincent placed a finger over her lips before she could finish.

"Now, now my dear. That is no way for a future Queen to speak," he said as he turned from her.

"Future queen my arse." Charlotte mumbled as she watched Vincent walk out of the cell.

Chapter Fifteen

Richard couldn't help but smile at the surprised look on his son's face. He also knew that Jordan would now be even more anxious to get Charlotte back. He wasn't surprised this had happened as Charlotte was now twenty-five and so was Jessica. This explained why the soul mate bond had finally kicked into place. However, there would have been some signs on Jordan's part when he had hit twenty-five.

Richard looked at both of his children. He knew that Jessica would have some questions and that Jordan's only care would be to get to Charlotte, but it wouldn't stop him asking.

"Questions anyone?" He needed something to take his mind off other certain revelations he had discovered.

"What?" Jordan snapped. "Are you kidding me???? Charlotte has been taken by an evil sadistic mongrel and you want to sit here all safe and sound and answer stupid questions."

"Are you King of the Elves?" Richard asked bluntly, giving his son a stern look.

"No."

"Right. So, until that time comes we will do things the way I see fit, understood." Richard spoke with the authority he had as the Elf King.

"Yes sir," Jordan replied realising that for a brief second it was not his father standing there.

"Good. I imagine there are a lot of questions and I will try and answer them all as best as I can. So, who wants to go first?" he said and looked towards Jordan.

"And no asking how or when we are going to get Charlotte back. Forewarned is forearmed. Jessica is going to need to know all she can especially if she is going to be coming back through with us. You my son don't know everything you need to know yet either. Any other questions in regards to Charlotte feel free to ask. I can imagine you are slightly confused as to what is going on there so we shall address that as well. Sound good."

"Yes father," Jordan replied. He figured that it would sound a little less sarcastic than dad would have. "But why are we not making up a battle plan to get her back? Instead of having a family history lesson. I know Jessica needs to know stuff but—"

"Jordan," Richard snapped cutting him off. "I know you want to get Charlotte back. I understand that because we all do. However, I have been a King for a very long time and have learned the hard way what happens to a person who doesn't know everything they need to. Which is why I'm cautious and try to gather all the information needed before I start to form it into a plan. Even the tiniest of details not known can de-rail the best of battle plans. Do you not recall what happened while getting you back? Now questions anyone?"

"I have one," Isabella said putting her hand up. He shot her a puzzled look. She looked towards Jordan, "What dreams?"

"What?" He looked at his mother with a puzzled expression.

"I read in the book something about dreams you were having of Charlotte while you were in the other realm."

"They don't mean anything."

Richard looked at his wife.

"Isabella where are you going with this?" He was genuinely interested. He was a King but he didn't know everything, especially about the other realms.

"I vaguely remember my dad saying something in regards to dreams, so I'm curious."

Jordan looked at his mother, "What do you want to know about them?"

"Just give me a brief synopsis on some of them."

"Ok then. Well I have dreamt of her loads. Almost every day in fact, thinking about it now."

"So, what happens in them?"

"It changes," he said shrugging. "Sometimes it's like I'm dreaming of stuff she's doing. Like working in a shop."

That caught Jessica's attention. "Really?"

"Yeah, that's when I'm not in the dreams with her. When I'm with her, I'm showing her around the Realms."

"You didn't introduce her to a woman called Trixie at all, did you?" Jessica asked.

"In one of the dreams I did," he frowned. "Why would you ask that?"

"I'll be back in a minute, don't say anything more until I get back." Jessica said as she bolted from the room. She returned a few minutes later with Charlotte's dream journal and handed it to her mother.

Isabella took the book from Jessica and started skimming through it. Her eyes were getting wider with every page. When she finished the book, she snapped it shut. "That's very interesting," she mused.

"What is?" they all asked at once.

"Wow, I got that in stereo."

"Mother," Jordan warned jokingly.

"Here. Have a quick read of this. I'm going to make some coffee," she said as she passed the dream journal to Jordan. She returned a couple of minutes later with the drinks and sat down. "Well what do you think?"

"There is stuff in here she couldn't possibly know. Other than that, it's practically identical with the dreams I remembered we were both in." Jordan replied, "Does she work in a shop that sells incense and crystals?"

"She actually owns it," Jessica replied with pride for her friend. "Her brother actually came over from America to help her set it up."

"Does Joanne know about the shop?"

"Yeah, she helps in the shop sometimes. Why?" Jessica asked.

"No reason," Jordan answered, not really wanting to open-up that can of worms. He had dreamt of her buying spell books.

"Ok, so what have we just discovered," Richard asked looking at each of them in confusion.

"Technically, Jordan and Charlotte have seen each other every day while he has been in the other realms. It was in dream form granted but it would seem that when they were asleep at the same time they would meet up. If only one was asleep then they would be dreaming of what the other one was doing."

"What gives you that impression," Richard asked.

"There is no way Jordan could know about Charlotte's shop. He had already gone to the realm when she got it and we wouldn't have told him. You heard him, there is stuff in her dream journal that she couldn't possibly know about him in those realms." Isabella explained.

"So, what does this mean?" Jordan asked.

"I have no idea. You have both been dreaming of what the other has been doing for five years and you were realms apart." Isabella slumped back into her chair completely baffled.

"Have we got any books on the family trees of the witches?" Richard asked.

"Only my family. Why?" Isabella replied.

"I remember Ruby mentioning something about dreams."

"Who's Ruby?" Jessica asked. "That's the second time you have mentioned her."

"An old friend," Richard said flatly. He looked at his wife when she giggled. "Now is not the time to go into who she is, we have more important things to discuss. Any questions?"

"What's the Call of the Rose?" Jessica asked at the same time Jordan asked his question.

"Why did Trixie say I was the only one who can find Charlotte?"

"One at a time please," Richard said looking at Jordan. "We will start with Jessica's question first and then yours." He looked at Jessica as he continued. "Where to start?"

Richard got comfortable and then began.

"The Call of the Rose is basically a summons. Each family has a different flower or symbol. I know an American chap that has a daffodil. So, thank your mother. It's because of her side of the family that we got the rose."

"Is that why we have a rose on the front door?" Jessica asked interrupting her father as he took a breath.

"Yes."

"Ok. Is there something wrong with that rose because I would swear that it had petals?"

"It probably did. The rose is magical and changes with the seasons. It also goes black when the call of the rose has been sent out," Richard explained.

"So how does all that work, with the rose and the house?" Jessica asked.

"As I have said, the house is magical—"

"You can't just say it is magical. There has to be some logical reason for it being the way that it is," Jessica interrupted again.

"There most likely is. However, that information has been lost to us for centuries, a millennium in fact. So, unless you know someone who is at the bare minimum a thousand years old if not older and was present at its conception you will just have to accept it's magical, got it."

"Sorry," Jessica said snidely.

"Now as I was saying," Richard said taking a furtive glance at his daughter. "It is connected to the Neutral Realm. A door way if you like, from this Realm to that. If any members of the royal families are in mortal danger it sends out a call. It calls back all its subjects from the Human Realm. For argument sake, when Jordan was taken by my brother he was put in mortal danger. Because he is Jordan, Prince of the Elves and next in line to the throne and I am King of the Elves I was automatically summoned back. Now if Charlotte, was put in mortal danger heaven forbid, I would once again be automatically summoned back, however this time so would Jordan."

"How come?" Jessica asked. Jordan just stared at his father not knowing what to say. "She isn't royalty."

"True and since Jordan has finally realised his part in all of this, I think that it's safe to say that Charlotte is his soul mate."

"Soul mate?" Jordan repeated raising a sceptical eyebrow at his father.

"Yes. Which is why you would be called and why Trixie told you that you are the only one who can find her."

"Ok so how long has everyone known about this?" Jordan asked glancing at each person in turn.

"Sweetie. We have known since you two were little." It was Isabella to speak this time. "You have always dropped anything you were doing to do as Charlotte asked."

"No, I haven't."

"Yes, you have. You would walk down to the shops in the pouring rain just because Charlotte asked you for some sweeties. You would come back with sweets for your sisters granted but if they had asked you to go, you would have just told them to get stuffed. If Charlotte wanted a bed time story when she slept over you would tell your mates you were going to be late and read her one. Even your sisters had that sussed out. If they wanted something they just got Charlotte to ask you."

"Fine whatever." Jordan had no other response to his mother's words. He had only just then realised how true they actually were. "So why am I the only one who can find her then?" Jordan asked his father.

"Can you feel Charlotte while you are sitting here?" Richard asked already knowing the answer.

Jordan closed his eyes trying to concentrate. He was getting mixed emotions, fear and anger and none of which were his. "I don't know. Why?" he asked looking at his father.

"Because, no matter what realm she is in you will be able to feel her and sense her."

"Would that work in reverse?" Jessica asked shakily.

"I don't see why it shouldn't, however it is not usually the case. Especially with a partial bond," Richard said looking at his daughter. "Why do you ask?"

"Well. There was this one time that Charlotte went through a couple of days of having no energy. I think at least twice she started screaming in pain and collapsing. The doctors didn't know why."

"When was this?" Richard asked her.

"When Jordan was in the other realm," Isabella answered.

"How do you know?" Richard said shooting his wife a look.

"Jessica called me about Charlotte just after you had gone to Rose Manor. Since I wasn't being granted access to the other realm I went to see the girls."

"Are you saying that there is a strong possibility that Charlotte felt everything that I felt when Vincent was torturing me?" Jordan asked. His blood pressure rising at the thought of it.

Richard was stunned, he didn't really know what to say. In all his years, he had never heard of such things happening. What was it about Jordan and Charlotte that the Fates decided to give them such a strong bond? It was the strongest to ever grace any realm and what else had they been blessed with?

"It would seem so," was all Richard could say to his son as he slowly sat in the chair behind him.

"What if Vincent starts to torture her like he did me?" Jordan asked through clenched teeth.

"Sweetheart. We have already said that Vincent is more than likely to seduce her," Isabella replied. She knew the words meant very little and wouldn't help the situation they were in. "Besides, you could always flash. How much energy does it drain from you when you do?"

"What? You've got to be daft! I can't flash. I'm of the Elfin Realm," Jordan said waving his hand theatrically.

"Isabella," Richard warned.

"Shut up Richard," she snapped giving him a filthy look and turned back to her son. "Jordan, you are also my son. This means you have Fae powers as well as some witch ones. Of course, you can flash."

"Isabella, now is really not the time—"

"Our son has been in the Elfin Realm for five years and nobody has told him he can flash. What? Did everyone conveniently forget that he has my blood in him too?" She was fuming at her husband once again for his lack of forethought.

"Isabella, it wasn't mentioned due to the fact that none of the elves can flash," said Richard as he stood. "Nobody would have been able to teach him how to use that power. Now he knows he has the ability he is going to want to use it to get Charlotte back."

Jordan's head shot up and the gleam in his eyes confirmed the thought had only now just crossed his mind.

"Oh great. Now I've gone and given him the bloody idea," Richard yelled waving his arm in the air. He turned to look through the glass doors that lead to the back garden.

"Mummy can teach me," Jordan said grabbing onto his mother's hand.

"Really? You're going to play the mummy card?" she said cocking her eyebrow at him. She looked down at her son's hand on hers. "I will teach you. However, not yet."

"Why? Damn it." Jordan stood in frustration and pulled back his hand.

"Because, I said so for one. Plus, it would take too much of your energy especially in your current condition."

"What condition?" Jordan bellowed.

"I don't know. Maybe the fact you can't control your emotions at the moment. Neither can you differentiate between yours and Charlotte's. Yes, you are of the Elfin Realm which means your elf powers would be stronger, but you are also part Fae. This means your energy will be drained quicker when you use that power."

"Like the Star Wars game?" Jessica asked.

"What?" Isabella asked turning towards her daughter.

"The Star Wars games. In one of them if a Jedi uses a dark power it consumes more of their Jedi power than a light side power would."

"And you know that how?" Isabella asked.

"Oh please, I'm always playing the light side. But I do love using the life drain ability, which is a dark power."

"Okay then," Isabella said as she turned back to Jordan. "Exactly what she just said."

"But mum, I feel fine," Jordan exclaimed. "And I promise not to flash to any other realms."

Isabella raised an eyebrow at her son. Did he really think she was going to believe the bullshit dribbling out of his gob?

"No. I will not teach you or tell you how to use that power. I don't want you to flash to your demise."

"You're being a little melodramatic. Don't you think?" Jordan said raising his eyebrows at his mother.

"No, I'm not." Isabella had never wanted to slap her son so much in his whole adult life. "You do not have the reserved energy it would take to flash. Even if you were in the Elvin Realm you wouldn't have the energy to flash from one castle to the next in your current condition. It would drain you and you would pass out. Some knight in shining armour you would turn out to be."

"That was a little harsh." Richard chimed in. He turned around and faced the room and had to hide a smirk at the stunned look on his son's face. Harsh or not, he had to admit that Isabella had made a good point.

"I don't care," Isabella stated. "It's the truth. Now on that note—I saw that look mister." she said pointing her finger at Richard before continuing. "It's getting late and I'm getting hungry. While I'm getting dinner ready you can take Jessica into the garden and teach her some elf stuff Richard, while there is still light outside."

She looked at Jordan. "You. Go and lay down for a little while."

"Why?" Jordan asked. "I told you I was fine."

"Jordan sweetheart, anyone who looks at you can see you are far from fine. Your energy is slowly draining from you even now. You have to deal with your own emotions as well as Charlotte's which is not an easy thing to do. Physically you may very well be fine, however emotionally and mentally you are not. In your current state, you would be of no use to Charlotte whatsoever. She will need your strength now more than ever to help her through this. Now go and get some rest. You have had a lot to deal with and it's taking its toll on you." Isabella said rubbing her hand on his cheek and placing a kiss on the other one.

"Fine." Jordan said in defeat. He placed a kiss on his mother's forehead and left the room.

Chapter Sixteen

Jordan slowly opened the door to his bedroom. He didn't want to sleep or get any rest when god knows what was happening to Charlotte but his mother had made a strong argument. What good would he be to Charlotte if he was exhausted? He couldn't control his emotions let alone distinguish between his and Charlotte's. All this confusion was not helping. It was clear he was of no use to anyone especially Charlotte. If he acted now it would most likely get himself or her killed, which was the last thing he wanted to do. He couldn't help wonder exactly how much energy flashing to her would really use up and did he really want to find out just yet?

Jordan laid down on his bed and placed his hands behind his head. He was thinking about what his parents had said and his own personal revelation. He was in love with Charlotte. Deep down he always had been and if it wasn't for his mother's persistence this afternoon he would no doubt, still be oblivious to it.

She was his soul mate, the love of his life. She would ultimately be his greatest weakness and he would bet his last pound that Vincent knew it.

Anger welled in him as he thought of his father's words earlier. Not his to have' and 'seduce her' where the phrases on repeat in his mind.

Vincent obviously wanted to use his feelings for Charlotte against him by seducing her. That was the only thing he could think of as to why Vincent would want her, except the fact that she wasn't his to have just like his father had mentioned. He would forever have the 'he had her first', hanging over his head. Could he handle that?

Sure, Vincent had screwed Sonya but Jordan had been done with her by then and his uncle had been welcome to his sloppy seconds. Just as Michael had been. But Charlotte was another matter entirely.

Just the thought of them in a lover's embrace was enough to make his stomach churn and his heart to ache. What if Vincent succeeded? The mere thought of that would have brought Jordan to his knees had he not been lying down. As it was all he wanted to do was roll on his side and curl up in the foetal position. If this was his reaction to thinking about such a thing happening what would he be like if it really did happen?

Despair and anguish consumed him and a single tear fell down his cheek. Not for himself but for Charlotte. The sweet innocent Charlotte he had always known. Hell, he didn't even know if she was still sweet and innocent anymore. He hadn't seen her in the flesh in five years not since his mishap and ending up in the Neutral Realm in the first place.

He didn't even know if Charlotte felt the same. He had always known just like everyone else that she'd always had a thing for him. Did she still feel the same? Had his absence made the heart grow fonder or had the feelings faded into nothing.

Either way, it wouldn't matter to Vincent. The vial creature that he is would still want to use her. Jordan knew Vincent didn't care for her, he didn't love her. She would mean nothing to him once he'd had her. She would be cast aside like last night's rubbish and for what? To punish and hurt him.

Jordan knew it would work. Just the thought of it felt like a knife had been plunged into his chest. Even breathing had suddenly become difficult to do. He really needed to get control of his emotions. It felt like they had gotten worse from the second he had put his head to the pillow. The sudden thought that after all these years he may have lost the woman he loved did not help him. Jordan climbed off the bed in frustration and went over to the window to look out over the garden. Winter had finally set in and the gloomy look of the sky and the bare oak tree in the garden was just making him worse.

Throwing himself back onto the bed he swore to himself that Vincent would not get the chance to use Charlotte at all. Somehow, some way, he would not let that happen. Not only for his sake but for hers. He just didn't know how he was going to prevent it. He would come up with something, he had too. Feeling more emotionally and mentally drained than before he finally closed his eyes and allowed his mind to wander to more pleasant thoughts of Charlotte until sleep finally consumed him.

Chapter Seventeen

Charlotte opened her eyes and found herself in a beautifully decorated red and gold room. From where she lay she could see lit candles in various places around the room. She thought the room was decorated for someone who had many a passionate night in mind. The black and red satin sheets she noticed she was lying on confirmed her thoughts.

She smiled remembering many a time she would fantasize being with Jordan in a room such as this. Realizing her arms were stretched out above her head she looked at the metal spiralled head board.

"Yep, many a fantasy." she said aloud noticing the hand cuffs attaching her to the bed. All she needed now was Jordan.

Suddenly remembering that Vincent had chained her up, she started to panic. She didn't know if this was real or she was dreaming. What if it was real? Was Vincent about to come through the door any minute to seduce her? She knew her heart belonged to Jordan as it always had. She would do what she could to avoid Vincent's advances but she had never been seduced before. What if she succumbed to his advances?

Fear crept its way into her stomach adding to the panic which had already settled there. Charlotte wriggled her hands and wrists to try and get out of the cuffs. The sound of someone clearing their throat made her stop dead in her tracks. She held her breath as she slowly looked towards the foot of the bed where the sound had come from.

Relief washed over her and she let out a breath she hadn't realised she had been holding. Her knight was standing at the foot of the bed looking delicious in jeans and a very tight t-shirt. His long hair was flowing just past his shoulders. "How long have you been there?"

"Long enough," Jordan answered as he walked around the bed to sit next to where she lay.

"Am I dreaming this?" she asked him.

"We both are," Jordan replied looking around the room they were in. "However, I think you are the one controlling the surroundings."

"Probably," said Charlotte blushing.

Jordan leaned over and brushed her check with his finger.

"My pretty one," he said smiling at her.

"You do know that is a title to a Cliff Richard song, don't you?"

"Is it?"

"Yes. I thought you were an AC/DC fan?"

"I am but growing up with my mother, her musical taste has rubbed off on me. Jessica isn't the only Cliff fan. Just don't tell anyone."

Charlotte looked at Jordan in stunned silence. Dream or no dream she would never have pegged him for a Cliff Richard fan, even a secret one.

Charlotte took a closer look at his face staring into his eyes. She had seen that look before, only this time it was more intense. There was definitely something different about him but she couldn't quite place what it was. Even the dream itself felt different to her not like the ones she had been having of Jordan for the past five years. She didn't understand why. Had something changed?

"Are you going to untie me?" she asked him. She was starting to get cramp in her shoulders.

"Not yet," Jordan teased smiling at her. "I quite like looking at you like this."

"Ok, what is going on? There is something different about this dream. It was nothing like the other ones and even having this conversation is different. What's that about?" Charlotte asked with worry.

Jordan looked at her. The dream did feel different but he figured it was because he knew he was finally seeing her. The fact he wasn't hiding his feelings was probably throwing her off as well. It was clear this was her dream. As romantic a setting this room was he was sure it wasn't from his mind. Her dream or not he was about to take control of it before time ran out.

"I'm controlling the dream," he said. Jordan laughed at the scowl on her face, she clearly didn't like that idea. "What do you remember from Rose Manor? After Jessica left."

"Why would you want to know that?" she said frowning at him.

"Humour me."

"Okay. I was brushing my hair in front of the mirror in your room when this dude in black grabbed me and pulled me through it. I mean seriously, how in the hell is that even possible? Wait. How do you know I was at Rose Manor?"

"What happened next?" Jordan asked deciding to avoid that question for now.

"Well the bastard chained me up. He didn't even want me, he was after Jessica. I was just there."

"Has he hurt you?" Jordan asked running his fingers through her blonde hair.

"Not yet. He just said he intends to seduce me to hurt his nephew."

"Did he say who his nephew was?"

"No. But he did say that Jessica was his niece," she said looking at him. "And I know that would make you his nephew. But as much as I would want to believe it's you he keeps referring I'm meant to be with, I couldn't bring myself to do it. So, I refused to assume it was you. Even more so when he didn't give me a name. I don't know this guy from a bar of soap. He could have a hundred nephews for all I know. Hell, I didn't even know your dad had any siblings."

Jordan smiled at Charlotte. He would let her know that he was his only nephew but not just yet.

"What do you intend to do when he makes his seduction attempts?" Jordan asked in disgust. Anger laced his words, he couldn't help it. Even in a dream the thought was eating away at him.

"What was that?" Charlotte asked noticing his tone of voice had changed.

"What?" he asked.

"That tone of voice you just used." She noticed the tone had more emotion in it than if he had of been asking one of his sisters that question.

"I don't like the thought of him using you like that." He placed his hand on her cheek and gently rubbed his thumb over it. "Now, what do you plan to do?"

"I don't know? Play along before kicking him in the bollocks."

Jordan couldn't help the chuckle that left his lips.

"Well try not to get yourself killed before I can get to you," he said only half joking.

"Please. He wants to seduce me, not kill me. Would be just my luck he would kill me while his nephew was watching."

Hearing those words sent Jordan's heart plummeting. He wouldn't put it past his uncle to do something like that. He felt the unease in his body and he knew he was about to wake up.

"Let's get you out of these cuffs." Jordan reached over her head and undid the hand cuffs placing them next to the pillow.

Jordan put his hands on either side of her face and bent down placing a gentle kiss on her lips. Leaning back to stare into her eyes he couldn't help but notice the surprised look on her face. Even in a dream she was breathtakingly beautiful and she was his.

"I will come for you," he said with determination.

Before Jordan knew what had hit him Charlotte wrapped her arms around his neck and was kissing him with such passion Jordan couldn't help the desire that swept through his body. He pulled her closer to him and placed a hand on her hip. He ran his other hand through her hair adding his own passion to their kiss. All the blood in his body heated and headed south arousing his manhood. As much as he would have loved to have stayed and made love to her all night, now just wasn't the time.

Feeling the pull to the waking world becoming stronger Jordan leaned back from the kiss, smiling at the disappointed look on Charlotte's face. Placing his hands once again on either side of her face he placed a small kiss on her nose and stopped leaving his face only inches from hers.

"Vincent only has one nephew," Jordan whispered as he gently placed his lips on hers and disappeared.

Charlotte looked at the empty space where Jordan had been.

"Now he wakes up," she said. She waved her arms in frustration before letting them slam back on the bed.

It suddenly dawned on her what his last words were. 'Vincent only has one nephew.' She couldn't help the surge of emotion that washed through her body enveloping her like a lover. She was going to have the man her heart desired.

Chapter Eighteen

Charlotte slowly opened her eyes feeling the intense emotions from the dream she had just had. Not only had the dream felt different to her, she couldn't remember ever having a dream where Jordan had kissed her. Smiling at the memory she slowly sat up. Looking at the cobbled stone floor she figured there was no point in trying to get comfy. Lifting her legs up and resting her arms on her knees she suddenly realised they felt lighter. The shackles were gone. She moved her wrists around, enjoying the feeling. She couldn't help but wonder how they came off. Her hands had not been small enough to fit through them, so why was she no longer wearing them.

Looking behind her, she spotted them lying beside the pillow where she had been sleeping. They looked suspiciously like they had been placed there. When she picked them up she noticed that they had, in fact, been undone.

"So, didn't slip off then," she said aloud as she examined the shackles. There was no visible way they would have come undone by themselves. Had someone come in while she was sleeping to undo them? And if so why?

Charlotte sat there contemplating possible reasons. "Ok Charlotte think. You wake up and the shackles are off. Is someone hoping that I try to escape? Was that Vincent's plan. Hunt me down like an animal and have his wicked way with me." Charlotte visibly shuddered at the thought and continued her musings.

"Well that couldn't be possible." Charlotte remembered that Jordan had undone the cuffs during the dream. "That was just a dream, wasn't it? Then again, I am in a dungeon and an elf-like creature wants to seduce me," she said sighing. "Let's just assume for arguments sake that currently anything is possible."

Shrugging at the thought Charlotte slowly got to her feet and rubbed her hands down the legs of her jeans. She could feel the effects of being chained all night and sleeping on the ground. Her body radiated small aches and pains all over. "Let's hope I'm not spending another night on that floor," she said rolling her head on her shoulders trying to ease her aching muscles.

She turned towards the door and wondered if it was even locked. She had seen enough movies to know that it would not be a good idea make an escape attempt. There was probably a guard on the other side of the door just waiting to zap her if she got out. She decided to walk over to the window to see what was outside and was surprised at the beautiful view.

"So not what I was expecting." Charlotte couldn't believe her eyes. Was she really looking at plush green grass? She was located in a castle about three stories up.

"Funny place for a dungeon. Unless it was used as a form of torture," Charlotte mumbled. Sadness overwhelmed her at the thought of all the poor souls who had seen this view and were never again free to enjoy it. Charlotte wiped the tear that fell on her cheek. She stood on her tiptoes and slowly leaned her head out of the window. It was more like a decorative hole in the wall than a window. It reminded her of the old medieval castles scattered around England.

She could see Vincent with a woman that was wearing something Peter Pan would. She wished she could hear what they were saying. She wasn't at the best angle to read their lips. Charlotte noticed another woman coming towards them. She looked like a servant and was carrying what appeared to be a covered tray of food. The servant passed the tray to Vincent and the other woman stamped her foot and stormed off. Charlotte watched as the woman stormed up the stone path which was surrounded by gorgeous green grass.

The sound of a key jiggling in the lock brought her attention back to the door. "Shit," Charlotte breathed out as she ran back to where the shackles were. She placed them over her wrists and waited for the person to enter.

Vincent walked into the room making sure he closed the door behind him and then turned to look at Charlotte.

"How did you sleep?" Vincent asked bringing the tray of food over to her. He placed the tray down on the floor just in front of her.

"I was on a stone floor with a crappy pillow and no blankets. How do you think I slept?"

"Were you cold at all?" Vincent asked.

"Surprisingly, no. But that's not the point," Charlotte replied before looking at the covered tray. "What's that?"

"That would-be breakfast. We can't have you going hungry. You were asleep when the evening meal was brought up to you." Vincent reached over and uncovered the food and placed it closer to her on the floor.

Charlotte looked down at the food. It smelled delicious. A full English breakfast with what smelt like a pot of coffee. "Is that coffee?"

"Yes."

"It's in a tea pot."

"There's a difference?" Vincent asked raising an eyebrow at her.

"Funnily enough, yes. I'll let you look that up," she said with a smirk. "What are you?" she asked as she wriggled her bum forward to get closer to the tray. She hadn't realised she was hungry until the food was brought in.

"I'm an elf. What would make you ask that now?" he said confused.

"Well I didn't think to ask that yesterday. I was in shock from being kidnapped but I've slept since then," she replied between mouthfuls of food. The bacon was so delicious it almost melted in her mouth. "So, are there witches and other things like that?"

"Yes." Vincent replied. He was slightly put off by how casual she appeared to be.

"Ok then."

"You don't appear to be shocked by that news."

"Please! I own a shop that sells spell books and stuff like that. Finding out witches and others things actually do exist, is no surprise to me. That stuff has to come from somewhere." Charlotte smiled at the bewildered look on his face.

"I will leave you to your breakfast," Vincent said as he turned around and left the room.

Charlotte noticed that Vincent hadn't locked the door. She must have totally rattled his cage for him to forget about that. She took the shackles from her wrists and continued to eat her food.

"No point wasting perfectly good bacon," she said as she leant her head back and popped it in her mouth. Even the coffee was divine. Just the way she liked it, with milk and sugar. She had expected black coffee with no sugar at the most.

She needed to wait a little while longer to be sure Vincent had gone before she made her escape. After polishing off her breakfast she decided that enough time had passed. She slowly walked up to the door, put her ear up to the solid wood and listened. Not being able to hear anything she stood on her tip toes to see out of the tiny four bared window. A dimly lit hallway greeted her and she noticed that there wasn't anyone on either side of the door. She slowly grabbed the large metal ring and turned it as she lifted the latch.

Her entire surroundings reminded her of a Robin Hood film. She would put money on the door being made of English oak as well. Pulling the door slightly ajar she waited for someone to come. When nobody came, she opened the door fully and cautiously looked out.

The corridors looked to be endless, fire blazed from the torches on the wall sconces. How more medieval could this place look? She was half expecting King Richard to come back from the crusades or at the very least Robin Hood and his Merry Men.

She had no idea how to get out of the castle, or which direction she should go in. Reaching into her jeans pocket she pulled out a small five pence piece.

"Heads left, tails right," she said as she tossed the coin in the air and caught it in her fist. She opened the palm of her hand and looked down. "Left it is then," she said as she walked out of the room and headed in that direction down the corridor.

Walking in high heel boots on a stone floor was not a great idea she thought as her heel slipped once more on the smooth edges of the stone. Charlotte put that thought out of her mind. She kept moving along the stone wall looking for anything that resembled a stair case. She knew at the very least, she had to head down to be able to get out.

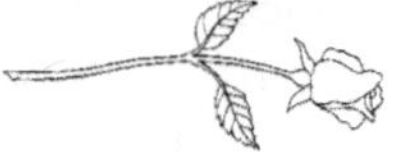

Vincent returned to the cell where he was keeping Charlotte. He was not at all pleased to find she was no longer there. He walked over to where she had slept and cursed under his breath as he knelt down and picked up the shackles.

"How the hell did she get out of these?" he demanded out loud to the empty room. He discarded the shackles on the floor and stood up abruptly. He was the only one with a key to her cell so nobody else could have gotten in and he sure as hell hadn't unchained her.

Did she have the shackles on when he brought her food this morning? He thought back to this morning as it hadn't been that long ago. He couldn't remember that but he did remember the open door. Why had he not locked the blasted door when he had left?

Vincent stepped out into the corridor, closed his eyes and sniffed the air. He could feel her in the castle, could still hear her heart racing. Hell, he could even smell the cherry blossom scent she was wearing as it still lingered. She indeed hadn't gone very far.

Turning left he slowly started heading in her direction. He knew he could just flash to her position or could use his power to place her in stasis, but where would be the fun in that.

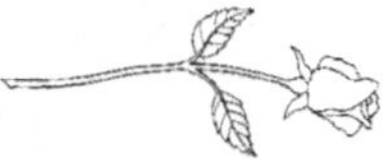

Charlotte had been walking along the corridor for a while trying every door she came across hoping it would lead her to some stairs. Stopping to try another locked door she heard foot steps behind her. Slowly taking in a deep breath she turned her head to see who was there. Her eyes widened with fear as she saw Vincent slowly walking up the corridor towards her. His arms were placed casually in front of his body and his hands were clasped together. It was just like the scene of a horror movie, where the killer stalked its prey down a dark alley.

Charlotte felt a surge of panic and she lost her footing, slipping on the stone. She could tell that she had damaged her ankle when she went down if the pain she felt was any indication. It wouldn't stop her though. Getting to her feet quickly she started hobbling along the wall. She used it to brace herself and tried to ignore the pain in her ankle. Pain that would shoot up her leg with every step she took. She felt just like a small animal being stalked by a predator.

She knew it wouldn't take Vincent much to catch up with her. She looked back at him she noticed that he hadn't changed the speed of his steps. They were still slow and a little too casual. The arrogance of the man infuriated her.

Deciding not to waste any more of her energy in a pointless escape attempt Charlotte stopped. The pain was slowly getting worse as her boot tightened around her ankle. She leaned her body against the wall and gradually slid down to the floor in exhaustion.

She leant her head back against the wall, closed her eyes in defeat and waited for her captor to reach her.

Chapter Nineteen

"Ok so what happened in the dream?" Richard asked Jordan after the breakfast things had been cleared away. They had decided to leave him sleeping the night before. Isabella had insisted because he had looked so peaceful.

"Is that really important?" Jordan asked as his mother and sister joined them at the dining room table.

"Considering what we discovered about your dreams with Charlotte, I think it is. You don't need to go into major details just give us the basics."

"Well she said that Vincent has her chained up and plans to seduce her to get to me," Jordan said looking at his father. "How the hell did you know he would try something like that?"

"Simple. Been there, done that. Kicked his arse because of it."

"He tried to seduce mum?"

"Yes, and he failed. Now let's change the subject. Did she say anything else?"

"She did say she would play along before kicking him where it hurts." Richard and Jordan both winced at the thought. "However, she didn't use those words."

"Not the best idea she could come up with. Elves are just as sensitive in that area as humans." Richard couldn't help wincing again. "What else?"

"Vincent informed her that she is meant to be with his nephew and that he was actually after Jessica."

"That doesn't surprise me…. hang on, where is Jessica? She was here a minute ago," Richard asked noticing his daughter was no longer in the kitchen with them.

"She has taken the dogs out for a walk. I think she needs some time to process things. She won't be long," Isabella answered.

"Ow. What the hell?" Jordan shouted as he reached down at the pain suddenly surging through his ankle.

"What is it?" Isabella asked rushing over to her son.

"I don't know. It feels like I just sprained my ankle. How is that possible? I'm sitting down, not moving," Jordan replied in confusion.

Richard leaned over the table and grabbed the book on Charlotte and skimmed to the last page. He couldn't believe what he was reading.

"This just can't be." Richard was so shocked by what he saw he was grateful he was already sitting down.

"What?" Isabella asked.

"Well, according to this book Charlotte has just sprained her ankle making an escape attempt." He passed the open book to his wife. Richard then turned his attention to his son. "You didn't say anything about an escape attempt."

"She didn't say anything. How was I meant to know she would try to escape?"

After reading the book, Isabella looked at her son. "Was Charlotte chained up at all in the dream?"

Jordan looked thoughtfully at his mother. "Yeah she was hand cuffed to a bed."

Isabella smiled when her son blushed. "Was she still hand-cuffed when you left the dream?"

"No. I un-cuffed her when I felt as though I was waking up, why?" he asked confused.

Isabella glanced towards her husband and couldn't hide the worry and confusion in her face. "I have to speak to my dad," she said and without another word she stood up and left the room.

"What's up with mum?" Jordan asked his father as his mother walked out the room.

"I have no idea. Can you please pass me the book on Charlotte?"

He passed the book to his father and sat in silence watching his father read the book. He was also waiting for his mother's return and he thanked god she hadn't gone shopping.

Chapter Twenty

A few hours later Isabella returned to the kitchen after talking to her father. Not only had it taken her a while to find him in the Witch Realm, but she also had to wait until his meeting had finished.

"What took you so long?" Richard asked and then noticed his mother-in-law behind his wife. "Christina what a surprise?"

"Richard darling," Christina said smiling. She walked towards him holding her arms out.

"What are you doing here?" Richard asked as he embraced his mother-in-law. He guessed she had gotten changed while they had been upstairs since she wasn't in her long silvery gown for the Fae Realm. She was dressed in black trousers and a white blouse. Her long white hair was as perfect as always.

"Well, Isabella told Tristan and me about the dreams Jordan and Charlotte seem to be sharing," Christina pulled out of her son-in-law's embrace and took a seat at the table. "Tristan has gone to consult the elders about it. He has his theories as to what it all means, not that he was sharing with me what it was mind you. He has gone to seek their council about it."

"Okay. So why are you here?" Richard asked, perplexed.

"Well I figured that Jessica was going to be a part of the rescue team and *you* can't exactly teach her to use all her magic at once. At best, all you can teach her is defence and how to attack with weapons. So, that is why I came through. Speaking of which, where are Jessica and Jordan?" Christina asked as Isabella placed a mug of tea in front of her. "Thank you darling," she said.

"They went out since we didn't know when you were getting back. I figured Jordan could use some fresh air and Jessica went with him.

Plus, with his impatience to rescue Charlotte I just couldn't focus on anything. He was doing my head in."

"Have you come up with a battle plan yet?" Isabella asked her husband.

"No, but we do have a few advantages. The book on Charlotte being one of them."

"There's a Realm book on Charlotte?" Christina asked with surprise.

"Yes," Richard replied handing her the book. "Why does it sound like it's an unusual occurrence?"

"Well it is and for her to have her own book means that she must have something to do with one of the Realms," Christina said touching her chin in thought.

"She is Jordan's soul mate." Isabella said helpfully.

"We already knew that darling," Christina said smiling at her daughter. "It would have to be more than that. Otherwise she would only be in the books on Jordan. So, she must have a blood connection to the Realms. That is the only reason I can think of as to why she has her own book," she said placing the book on the table. "I bet your father knew that already."

"Could Charlotte be related to us through Dad?" Isabella asked her mother.

"No, your dad would have known if she was. However, there is more than one family of witches. Charlotte could be a descendant from one of the ones we know or related to a completely different branch of supernatural beings."

"Like what?" Isabella asked.

"I don't know it could be any number. Pixie's, wolves, goblins, vampires, leprechauns, Unicorns and that's to name a few. Pick one," Christina replied shrugging her shoulders. She turned her attention back to Richard. "So, what other advantages have we got?"

"The dreams that Charlotte and Jordan keep having," Richard replied.

"As I understand it, Jordan and Charlotte have been meeting while dreaming. I know that Jordan is aware of it, but is Charlotte?"

"No and with her making that escape attempt," Richard said standing and rubbing his chin in deep thought. "That really could have stuffed up any rescue mission." The sound of laughter grabbed his attention and made him look up.

"I'm sorry my dear. You always take forever to come up with a battle plan," Christina said trying to muffle her laughter with her hand and failing.

"And yet how many deaths stain my hands?" Richard asked giving her a stern look.

Christina looked at him thoughtfully.

"Point taken. You have always taken forever to come up with a plan. You always make sure you know everything there is to know and have every angle covered. There aren't many who have died in your command. Well, except in that one battle."

"That was the first battle I was in when I became King. If you recall, the elves got ambushed and it ended up being a massacre and not in our favour. I swore then it would never happen again."

"What battle?" Isabella asked.

"The Battle of the Realms," Richard replied.

"When was that?" Isabella asked, she didn't recall ever hearing about it. Not even during her mother's famous stories.

"Many moons' ago," Christina replied.

"Mother."

"Fine then, it was a very long time before you were born. Your brother Theodore was about five at the time."

"Wasn't that the battle that David and Constance died in?" Richard asked.

"Yes. Thank you for that memory," Christina snapped.

"Who are David and Constance?" asked Isabella not sure she had ever heard those names before. She had also never seen her mother react like that before.

"Well, Constance was Vincent's soul mate and David's twin sister." Christina looked at Isabella with pain filled eyes. "They were also your older siblings."

"Come again," was all Isabella could respond with. She wasn't entirely sure she had heard her mother correctly.

Chapter Twenty-One

Charlotte couldn't believe that Vincent was yet again chaining her up. He had chained her standing up and with a sprained ankle no less. Glancing around the cell, she didn't see anything that looked familiar. He had obviously placed her in a different one from the one before. She couldn't help noticing that this one had been damaged. One side of the wall looked slightly different to the rest like it had to be repaired or rebuilt.

Her arms had been chained above her head and the shackles around her wrists were not only heavy but seemed to have had rope or something added to them. These ropes were cutting into her wrists. She wasn't surprised since by the look of things she could have easily slid out of the shackles themselves. She was glad he hadn't used cheese wire or something more torturous to keep her in place. To avoid further pain she grabbed onto the chain relieving some of the pain in her ankle. The pain was close to unbearable now as her foot continued to swell in the confines of her shoe. She hoped it wouldn't cause serious lasting damage or cause her to lose her foot or even her leg. Was that even possible?

Taking her mind off the pain for a moment she noticed that Vincent hadn't moved since he had chained her up. His body was uncomfortably close to hers, even more so in this position which made her breast stick out. She wasn't a big girl in that department, but she wasn't small either. She froze when Vincent bent his head down into the crook of her neck. His body dangerously close to her chest.

Hearing him sniffing her sent an unwelcome shiver down her spine. Was that a sensitive part of a woman's body? She didn't know.

His head moved so his lips were next to her ear and she could feel his warm breath caressing her skin.

"How did you get out of the other chains?" Vincent asked seductively before gently blowing on her ear.

Charlotte closed her eyes and bit her lower lip trying to ignore the pleasant sensations running through her body. Obviously, it wasn't what he said, but how he said it. She regained her composure and replied. "I don't know?" she said and jumped when Vincent suddenly leant back to look at her.

"What do you…?" he started in an angry tone and quickly stopped himself. He changed his tone to a more seductive one. "What do you mean you don't know?" he said gently running a finger across her jaw line and over her lips.

"Exactly what I said, I don't know how I got out of them. I woke up and they were undone and placed next to me," Charlotte replied.

"Well they couldn't have come undone on their own," Vincent replied inching his head closer to hers.

Charlotte watched Vincent closely noticing that he was slowly moving his head closer to hers as though he was planning to kiss her. She couldn't stop herself from wondering if he was a good kisser and mentally scolded herself for the thought. She tried to focus her attention on other things. Her dream popped into her head and she tried to remember what she told Jordan she would do if he tried to seduce her. She had said she would play along before kneeing him. Well that part might be out of the question with a swollen ankle but she was sure she could come up with something. She just hoped she could resist and not give into any desires she may get.

"Have you been with anyone before?" Vincent asked. He heard the small pleasurable groan come from Charlotte's throat as he gently ran his finger tip down her neck.

"No, I haven't," Charlotte replied in a breathier voice than she would have liked. A sly smile crept across Vincent's lips. "What are you smiling about?"

"Seducing you may not be as hard as I first thought."

Charlotte just looked at him. *'Yeah that's right buddy, insulting me is a sure way of not getting what you want'* she thought as a small smile crossed her own lips.

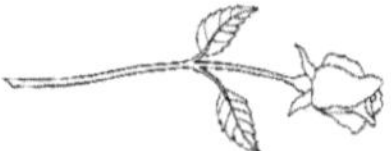

Vincent bent his head to steel a kiss from the beauty chained before him. His lips connected to hers and he motioned with his tongue for her to give him access. She obliged without hesitation. Vincent slipped his tongue deep into her mouth and wrestled her tongue with his own. He was enjoying the moment and how much this kiss would hurt his nephew. He didn't get to enjoy the thought for long as he realised the kiss was now only one way.

Not removing his mouth from hers he slowly opened his eyes and was greeted with the woman's. Her bright blue eyes had an evil gleam in them that had him cautious. He felt the sides of her mouth lift and he quickly pulled away from her. It wasn't quick enough and he was almost blinded by the excruciating pain that pierced through him. He subconsciously rubbed the back of his hand over his mouth certain he could taste blood. When he looked at his hand he couldn't miss the crimson liquid which was smeared there and probably all over his face. Vincent spat the blood from his mouth and glared at Charlotte. The defiant look on her face filled him with rage.

"YOU BITCH," he snarled and back handed her so hard it knocked her out cold. Her body swung slightly in the chains. Looking at her hanging there he wondered if she would get out of these chains as easily as she had the previous ones. With the addition of the shackles to keep her in place, he didn't think so. Vincent winced when he spotted the thin trail of blood flowing down her arm and onto her chest from the fat lip he had just given her. Damn it! Why did he keep doing that?

She was definitely more interesting to look at than his nephew was when he was hanging in the same place. She was a feisty, stubborn woman, even with her innocence. It was not going to be as easy as he first thought although he was going to have fun making her succumb to her desires. It would be a pleasurable task as long as he had the time he needed to seduce her. As it was, he knew it wouldn't be long before his brother and nephew came banging down his door to get her back.

She was his prize and he wasn't giving her up without a fight. Especially since his seduction plans have not yet come to fruition. As good as he was in that department, a little help wouldn't go astray. Walking towards the metal basin he had used many times before he slit his palm with the dagger he had hidden in his cloak and watched as his blood flowed into the bowl. Placing his index finger into the bowl he began to swirl the thick red liquid around.

"Ruby. I SUMMON THY," he boomed. He felt a breeze fill the room and he spun around to see a beautiful woman in a long fitted red velvet dress. The dress showed off the contours of her body.

"Sapphire?" whispered the woman.

"What?" Vincent said not quite catching what she said.

"Nothing," she said shaking her head. Ruby took in her surroundings. "Still into whips and chains I see."

"Ruby my love, you know me," he said as he walked towards her.

"What do you want?" she said in anger.

"Did I interrupt you again with one of your many lovers, my love?"

"Not this time," she said as she remembered the last time he had summoned her to the dungeon. With that in mind she turned her attention to the unconscious woman chained in the middle of the room.

"Who is that?" she asked him.

"Jordan's soul mate," Vincent replied.

"What's her name?" Ruby asked as she headed towards the unconscious woman.

Vincent stared blankly at her. "I don't actually know."

"Where did you get her from?" Ruby asked as she slowly started to circle the girl. She was hardly a girl even Ruby could see that.

"The Human Realm. I just grabbed her and pulled her straight through the mirror," Vincent said with a huge smile on his face. He was clearly proud of his actions.

Ruby glared at him as disgust coursed through her veins.

"Let me guess. You were after your niece?" Vincent nodded. "But you ended up with a much better prize. What do you intend to do with her?"

"I have attempted to seduce her. My charm doesn't seem to be working as well as I'd have hoped," Vincent said as he rubbed his chin.

"Your charm not working? That's never happened before," Ruby's voice was thick with sarcasm. "Oh wait. You did fail to seduce Isabella and as I recall Richard went to town on your arse."

"You find great pleasure in bringing that up, don't you," Vincent said giving her a filthy look.

"Of course, my love. I have always loved watching your brother kick your arse, you know that." Smiling at the anger she could see in his face Ruby turned her attention back to the young woman. "Has she always been in these chains?"

"No. She escaped from the other chains she was in. I don't know how she did it, apparently neither did she."

Ruby looked at her and smirked. She knew exactly how the young woman had gotten out of the chains. Noticing the necklace used for draining power was not on her Ruby guessed that Vincent couldn't sense what little power this woman currently had. Considering what he had done to his nephew she wasn't about to let him do the same to her sister's descendant.

"What are you smirking at?" Vincent asked her suspiciously.

Ruby looked at him before answering. "I take it you have been trying to seduce her while chained up?"

"Yes…Why?"

"Words lose their charm when whispered through prison bars."

"What?"

"Nothing," she said in frustration. Why couldn't he be more like his sister? "Why did you call me?"

"I require your help with her."

"What do you want me to do?" Ruby said in complete shock. "I can't shield her from Jordan. You know as well as I do, being her soul mate he will find her no matter where you take her. Hell, being part Fae he could just flash straight to her."

"What *can* you do then?" Vincent said infuriated. He had completely forgotten Jordan had that ability. Naturally.

Waving her hand in the air she lowered the chains the young woman was being held up by. She watched the woman's limp body slowly slide to the ground and turned to face Vincent.

"Nothing. When it comes to this one you are on your own. But I will say this. I really don't think that she's *that* into whips and chains." Ruby smiled at him, clicked her fingers and disappeared.

Vincent stood there totally dumbfounded. He had spent so long indulging himself in sexual activity with women chained up that it hadn't occurred to him she may not actually be into that sort of thing. It was no wonder his seducing techniques weren't working. Hell, could he even remember how to seduce a woman that wasn't in chains?

Releasing her from the chains, he gently picked her up and carried her out of the dungeon. He needed a new seduction plan, and fast.

Chapter Twenty-Two

Charlotte slowly opened her eyes and was slightly confused with her surroundings. She was lying in a dark wood four poster bed that was surprisingly very comfortable. Green velvet curtains hung from every corner of the bed and the pillows were soft and plenty. She tried to sit up but she realised that her leg had been elevated with what looked like a sheet hanging from the top bed rail. She noticed her foot had been put in a bandage. It still looked to be slightly swollen but no longer hurt. She figured she could probably walk on it a little. Sitting up she gently took her foot out of the sling. Dangling her legs over the side of the bed she just sat there not knowing what to do next and looked around the room.

It was a rather lavishly decorated dark green and gold room. It looked as though it had a connecting bathroom, from where she sat. She could clearly see the toilet from the open door. All the wood furnishings in the room were a dark. She wasn't sure if it was the wood itself or because it had been varnished to give it that look. The bedside table was also a dark wood and had a beautiful golden coloured lamp with green glass placed atop it. Charlotte would swear it was one of those touch lamps.

Next to the bed side table was a dark wooden arm chair. It had dark green velvet cushions and gold studs imbedded in the velvet area around the edges. It reminded her of the chair set her Grandmother kept by the fire place on the occasions she had visited with her parents. The white folded items she saw on the seat stood out against their green back ground yet she hadn't noticed the items straight away.

Reaching over from where she sat Charlotte grabbed the white material and placed it on her lap. A smaller piece of white fabric fell to the floor with what looked like a folded piece of paper attached to it. Resting her weight on her good foot and bracing herself with her arm she bent down to recover the fallen items. She placed what looked like underwear on the bed and opened the folded piece of paper and began reading.

To the one I desire,

Please find with this note a change of clothes. Feel free to use the bathroom amenities to freshen up. There is a pair of crutches under the bed to assist you should you need it. I will be by later with your evening meal.

Vincent

Charlotte scoffed at the note. She felt slightly insulted by the fact he didn't even know her name. Retrieving the crutches from under the bed she slung what looked like a long night dress over her shoulder and slid the underwear around her wrist as she made her way to the bathroom.

Opening the bathroom door sometime later, Charlotte was surprised and not at all pleased to find Vincent sitting in the arm chair next to the bed. He was wearing a suit and it was flawless. It didn't have a crease in it, not even from his legs being folded. His long black hair was neatly tied back at the nape of his neck and he looked extremely relaxed.

"What do you want?" she asked not hiding her anger for him.

"I have brought you your evening meal," Vincent replied as he stood up. "Here, let me assist you."

"You can just stay where you are," she said pointing at him as best she could with her arms in crutches.

"You appear to be angry with me," Vincent said stopping his advance toward her.

"Really, whatever would give you that idea?" Charlotte said sarcastically.

"Well the tone of your voice to start with," Vincent replied.

"It was a rhetorical question, you moron," Charlotte snapped.

Vincent looked at her. "What did I do, that has made you so angry?"

Charlotte looked at him totally gobsmacked that he even had to ask.

"Let's forget about the kidnapping and chaining me up part of things for a minute shall we and focus on the other facts right now. Ohh I don't know something like, you slapped me and knocked me the fuck out you prick."

"Well you bit me and drew blood."

"You shouldn't have stuck your tongue in my gob without permission. So, suck it up princess," Charlotte replied and headed toward the bed with her dirty clothes draped over her shoulder.

Vincent stood there in shocked silence. Very few women would dare to speak to him like this woman just did. He was clearly going to have to do some serious grovelling. It had been a long while since he'd had to do anything of the sort.

"What are you smiling about?" Charlotte asked him.

"I was just remembering my soul mate. You reminded me of her."

"You have a soul mate?"

Charlotte was surprised to hear that and at the same time wondered why he was trying to seduce her. Did they have one of those open relationships? She hadn't thought too much into it but he didn't seem the type to her.

"Had." The pain he felt still laced his voice even after almost a century. "She died."

"Oh, I'm sorry for your loss." Charlotte stared at him in sympathy. She hadn't expected that. "How did she die?"

"She was in the wrong place at the wrong time," Vincent replied. "Look I am sorry for what I did, there is no excuse. I have never had that happen to me before and I automatically reacted."

Vincent really hated grovelling. Being a gentleman in any sense of the word was something he hadn't been in a very long time. Hell, he hadn't exactly been *a gentleman* to Sonya. Even when she had been in this very castle or when he spent a miserable six months in the Human Realm with her regaining his powers and avoiding his brother. His attraction to Sonya had been purely physical and he had used that to his full advantage. At least that's what he kept telling himself. Even now arousal stirred within him at the mere thought of the woman.

Charlotte looked at him maybe a little too closely. She could hear the sincerity in his voice however she wasn't entirely convinced. The glazed look she could see in his eyes did intrigue her. "Charlotte," she said as she remembered the note he had written.

"What?" Vincent asked in confusion. He'd been so lost in his thoughts he hadn't caught what she said.

"My name is Charlotte. I believe it is customary to know a person's name, especially if your intentions are to bed her. Unless of course it's just a one-night stand, then who cares about names right," Charlotte finished with a shrug.

"Quite." Vincent said just staring at the woman.

"Now. Where's this grub?"

How the hell could one woman baffle him so much? It was like she had a hidden mood switch he couldn't find. He was going to have fun seducing her and if nothing else, she would keep him on his toes.

He walked slowly over to Charlotte and stopped at her side. He grinned slightly as he picked her up and carried her out of the room to where he had food waiting.

Chapter Twenty-Three

Richard, Isabella and Christina all jumped at the sound of the front door slamming. They could hear Jessica yelling and Jordan trying to calm her down.

"When the hell—" Jessica couldn't remember anything she had been about to yell. Her grandmother sitting at the kitchen table had startled her into silence. "OH MY GOD." Well almost.

"Not quite," Christina answered getting up to give her shocked grand-daughter a hug.

Jessica started crying, she didn't know what to think or what to believe. "Are you really here?"

"Yes darling," Christina said smiling. She wiped away the tears that didn't seem to want to stop. Jordan walked over to his grandmother to greet her.

"Hi Nan," he said placing a kiss on top of her head. "Come on you," he said as he grabbed Jessica's hand and led her over to a chair at the table. He could see clearly that his little sister had gone into shock. He was expecting her to have a mental breakdown. He would probably find her in a dark room later rocking back and forth muttering to herself. Smiling at that thought, he took a seat next to his sister.

Richard waited for everyone to be seated around the table before he decided to address the group. He still hadn't come up with a battle plan and was beginning to think he needed to meet with his generals. Jessica was not ready to go through to the other realm yet so that idea would have to wait. Richard believed Charlotte was in no immediate danger and until such time as the call of the rose started, he would do what he did best and take his time strategizing.

"Are we all sitting comfortably?" Christina said. "Then we shall begin."

"Really mother, must you?" Isabella said scolding her mother.

"What I'm just trying to lighten the mood. Jordan will end up sending his father to an early grave if he continues to pester him about rescuing Charlotte and poor Jessica over there looks like she is about to have a nervous breakdown. You did tell her I wasn't actually dead, didn't you?"

"Yes mother."

"Good. So, Jordan where did you two go. Anywhere nice?" Christina asked.

"We went to Charlotte's shop and bumped into Joanne while we were there. I also picked Charlotte up a little something," Jordan said as he passed his grandmother the paper bag. Looking at his mother he continued. "I'm going to have to pay Janice a visit, aren't I?"

Not that it bothered him that much. He had missed all his sisters terribly while he had been stuck in the Elvin Realm.

"Yep. You know the second you left that shop, Joanne would have been on the phone," Isabella replied smiling at her son.

"I will pop down to her place tomorrow afternoon," he told his mother and then looked at his father. "I take it the rescue mission isn't planned as yet?"

"No. However, while you are visiting Janice tomorrow it would be a good opportunity for your grandmother to teach Jessica how to use her powers." Richard was starting to get a little worried about his daughter. She hadn't moved or said anything since Jordan placed her in the seat. She hadn't even blinked and just seemed to be transfixed on her grandmother. Richard noticed that didn't seem to bother Christina in the slightest which infuriated him but he just clenched his teeth and said nothing.

"Jordan sweetie, why did you get this for Charlotte?" Christina asked holding up the rose quartz heart pendant.

"I see it and thought of her. So, I grabbed it," he replied with a casual shrug. He watched his grandmother cup the pendant with her hands and speak words into it. "What are you doing?"

"Just blessing it dear," she said passing the necklace back to him. "It's very lovely."

"Thanks," he said as he took the necklace from his Nan and placed it in the inside pocket of his favourite leather jacket. He hadn't seen it in five years and was in no hurry to take it off as yet. "Do you think she is alright?" he asked nodding his head towards his sister.

"I imagine she will be fine once she gets over the initial shock." Christina glanced briefly at Jessica then turned her attention back to her grandson and frowned. "What was she doing her nut over when you guys came home?"

"Well. We were chatting about when I went to the other realm. The subject of me not being able to come back for five years came up."

"And?" Christina said motioning for him to continue.

"I mentioned how I'd been stuck there."

"So, she was doing her nut over the fact that once she goes through she will be there for five years."

"Yeah," Jordan replied with a cheeky smile on his face.

"Well, maybe she can request an audience with the elders and ask them for a small reprieve before she has to go through?"

"How come she gets that option and I didn't." Jordan enquired and tried not to scowl at his grandmother.

"Jordan darling, she would still have to do her five years in the Realm of the Fae. However, due to the situation and why she is going through early they may grant her a little time to get her affairs in order."

"Oh, okay then. So why didn't I get that option? After all, I did end up there sooner than I should have"

"You being slightly clumsy wouldn't merit you an audience with the elders," Christina stated smiling sweetly at her grandson. She remembered how he'd ended up in the realm sooner than planned.

"Right. Well on that note, I'm going down to the chip shop to get dinner," he announced as he stood up.

"Do you have any money?" asked Isabella. "Your bank cards and things would have expired by now. I dare say you probably left your credit card with Trixie."

"Most definitely mother. I popped into the bank while Jessica and I were out and it would seem that in my five-year absence, my books have done rather well." He placed a kiss on top of his mother's head. "I'll be back soon."

Chapter Twenty-Four

"Where did Jordan go?" Jessica asked suddenly when she heard the sound of the front door closing. It made everyone at the table jump.

"He's gone to get dinner," Isabella said to her daughter.

"Oh. What are we having? Anything nice?" she asked staring out at nothing. Her face was void of any emotion.

"Fish and chips."

"Oh okay, that's nice. I hope he remembers I have a battered sausage with my portion of chips."

"I'm sure he will," Isabella replied smiling at her daughter.

"Here we go gathering nuts in May on a cold and frosty morning," Jessica started singing while tracing the patterns on the table cloth with her finger tip.

"Jessica?" Isabella said and placed her hand over her daughters to stop it from tracing. "Are you alright?"

"No Mummy," Jessica replied sounding exactly how she felt. Like a lost little girl.

"Jessica darling. Tell mummy how you're feeling." Isabella knew that it was probably a little redundant asking her such a thing but figured if she got Jessica to talk about what was on her mind she would snap out of it.

"Tell you how I feel?" Jessica said turning her head towards her mother. "That's just it Mother, I don't know how I feel. In the past three days, my life has been totally turned upside down. To start with my grandmother who I thought was dead for six years had actually been alive and well the whole time and living in another Realm.

"Then my brother who was missing for five of those years had actually been stuck in another Realm. My best friend has been kidnapped by some looney who wants to seduce her and I don't know why. To get at my brother? I mean seriously what the hell did Jordan do to him? From what I've read and been told so far, its Jordan who should be seeking revenge for the torture he endured. I mean going to get my best friend back is a given. I would walk to the ends of the earth for her. But finding out that once I go through to get her I am stuck there for 5 years. Please mother, please tell me exactly how I am meant to feel because I really just don't know."

"Feel better now you had that little vent?" asked Isabella.

"Yeah, I do now you mention it," Jessica replied feeling a little less heavy hearted. "So, Nan, what brings you here?"

"Well. Someone needs to teach you how to use your powers," Christina said.

"What powers?"

"You, like your brother, have powers."

"What about Janice and Joanne?" Jessica asked intrigued.

"Um…. Feel free to chime in at any moment," Christina said looking from Richard to Isabella and back again.

"You are on your own with this one. As you pointed out, I can only teach my daughter the weapon side of things," Richard said while smirking at his mother-in-law.

"Right. Well you and all your siblings have powers of some form. Technically you all have the same powers. However, Jordan's Elf powers will be stronger since he is in the Elfin Realm. Where your Fae powers will be stronger since you are to go the Realm of the Fae. Your sisters also have powers but until they hit twenty-five it is unknown which ones they are going to be exactly.

"Now a quick Fae power lesson. Like with every species on the planet there is a way to defend and attack. The hardest part for you to learn will be to control and focus. Yes, we want to get Charlotte back but until The Call of the Rose has started we need to assume we have a little time."

"Why would The Call of the Rose be set off for Charlotte? I get that it's a royal family alert system and that Charlotte is Jordan's soul mate. But they aren't even together."

"That's exactly why. With your brother being Prince of the Elvin Realm and future King and a soul mate once found is a precious gift that has to be protected. As the future Queen of the Elves she will be the one to bring the next heir into their world."

"That sounds so old fashioned and medieval." Even as Jessica said it she thought it was kind of romantic. She had an overwhelming urge to go and read one of Charlotte's historical romances.

"What can I say? Men." Christina said raising her arms in a shrug. "Now back to what I was saying. Tomorrow while Jordan is visiting Janice I will give you a crash course on what your powers are and how to use them. Now bear in mind that in the Human Realm the powers are not as strong. This makes it the perfect conditions to teach you the basics. With me so far?"

"I think so," Jessica replied. "How come Dad can't teach me to use the powers?"

"He is an Elf and has different powers to those from other realms. You do have Elf powers. However, they will be dormant until you enter their Realm."

"Oh, ok fair enough then, that makes sense I guess." Jessica scrunched up her nose as she turned to look at her father. "This Vincent guy who has taken Charlotte."

"What about him?" Richard said with no emotion.

"He's your brother, isn't he? The same guy in that leather book that write's itself on Jordan?"

"Yes." Richard deadpanned. He was dreading where this little conversation might be going.

"Seriously, what the hell is his problem? I mean he takes Jordan and tortures him and then takes Charlotte and plans to seduce her to get at Jordan. What the hell did Jordan do to him?"

"Jordan did nothing except be born," Richard replied bluntly and sighed. "Vincent is selfish and self-centred, always has been."

Christina clamped her mouth shut and she noticed so did Isabella. Her son-in-law really did have a selective memory where his brother was concerned.

"You really need to smack your brother about a bit."

"I'll get right on that. Just as soon as we have finished our dinner," Richard replied hearing Jordan closing the front door and the smell of food drifting through the house.

Chapter Twenty-Five

Jordan hadn't realised how much he had missed English fish and chips while being in the Elvin Realm. All he had wanted to do once he had finished was go to bed and meet up with Charlotte. He'd even had to argue the point with his family when he told them he was going to bed.

His grandmother had said. "All work and no play will make Jordan a grumpy bum."

His father's comment was diplomatic. "Charlotte is in no life-threatening danger."

However, it was his mother's argument that had made sense. "She won't even be asleep yet so you may as well watch some tele."

So, Jordan had reluctantly followed everyone into the lounge room and watched a bit of television with the family. Not that he had actually been watching it. He'd spent the whole time playing with the necklace he had gotten for Charlotte. He knew it was ridiculous buying her something from her own shop, but he thought of her the second he saw it. It had been Joanne to suggest he get it for that reason and not because it was a sale.

Hearing the chimes of Big Ben on the tele he decided it was now time to go to bed. He was sure he'd get no arguments this time. Placing a kiss on the heads of each woman in the room he wished them all a good night before leaving. His dad had already fallen asleep in the big arm chair in the corner.

Reaching his bedroom, he slowly opened the door and didn't bother to turn the light on as he made his way to the bed. Laying down he noticed a small beam of moon light filtering into the room by a crack in the curtain. He figured it was a full moon outside. He held the necklace up and dangled it in the beams of moon light and watched the light catch it.

He didn't doubt he would dream of Charlotte. He had done so every day since he had gone to the other realm. So, why would tonight be any different? He still wasn't happy that they had not yet made an attempt at getting her back but it wasn't as yet his call to make.

Getting himself comfortable he closed his eyes and cleared his mind. Keeping his tumultuous emotions at bay he slowly drifted off into a deep sleep, the necklace against his chest and close to his heart.

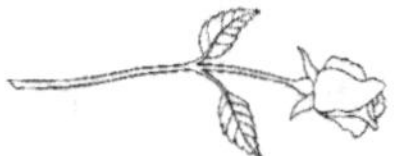

Jordan awoke to Charlotte lying on her side with her head resting on her hand just smiling at him. Not knowing quite what to think he blinked his eyes a couple of times. From where he lay he could tell he was still in his bedroom at Rose Manor. Did she escape from Vincent's clutches? Had his dad gone and gotten her without him? Was she dead and her ghost was paying him a last visit? So many questions were going through his head at once. He was fearful, especially thanks to his last thought. Jordan closed his eyes as realisation sunk in, he must be dreaming. Noticing the necklace still clutched in his hand put his mind in doubt yet again.

"Is this a dream?" Jordan asked. Charlotte just smiled at him and he didn't know if she actually was a ghost or not now. A giggle brought him out of his thoughts and diverted his attention back to her. He could see she had enjoyed watching him squirm. "That wasn't funny."

"Yes, it was," she said giggling again. "Your face was a classic. What, did you think I was a ghost of something?"

"The thought did cross my mind."

"Yes, I think so," said Charlotte suddenly.

"What?" Jordan asked. He was totally confused as to where that had come from.

"In answer to your question, yes I think this is a dream." She looked around before she continued. "However, I think this is your dream."

"What makes you say that?"

"We are in your room. As well as the total confusion on your face when you opened your eyes and saw me here."

"So, you're invading my dreams hey?" he said. He smiled and tickled her enjoying the sound of her laughter.

"Stop it," wheezed Charlotte after Jordan had finished tickling her. She looked him straight in the eye trying to work out what was happening between them. "What is going on?"

"What do you mean?" Jordan responded moving onto his side to see her better. They were now face to face with only a foot of space between them.

"This," she motioned between the two of them with her hand. "And everything else."

"Define everything else?" Jordan said scanning her face for anything that would indicate she thought this wasn't a dream. Not that he knew if he should tell her or not.

"Well to start with," she said as she sat up on the bed and folded her legs beneath her. "The dreams. The ones I have been dreaming of you for the past five years. They began when you went missing. Granted those dreams were weird enough on their own, what with being in a different realm. Since I got dragged into one I can believe that those had been actual places and not something my imagination had cooked up." She tilted her head to look at his face from where he was laying. "Are you a Prince?"

"Technically." It was all Jordan could say not letting his gaze shift from her eyes.

"So, that Prince Jordan of the Elves book that Jessica and I came across in the library. Which I might add started writing itself while I was holding it. That's on you, isn't it? Not someone your mum named after you."

"Yes," Jordan answered as he sat up. He turned on his backside so his whole body was facing her and folded his legs under him. He grabbed her hand and just held it not knowing what else to say.

Swivelling her entire body to face him, she continued. "How long have you known you were a Prince?"

"I found out not long after I went through to the Neutral Realm."

Charlotte looked at him and raised her eyebrow. "You fell through a mirror."

"Didn't I say that?"

"Your wording implied you went through on your own accord."

"A minor technicality," Jordan replied waving his hand at her words. "Did you really think I was an idiot for that?" he asked remembering what his sister had said.

"What?" she said in confusion. "No. Hang on, did Jessica say I did?" Jordan nodded. "Little cow."

"So, what else is troubling you my love?" Jordan had known Charlotte a long time and he could tell by the look on her face there was something more to her worries. He winced at the shocked look on her face at his slight faux pas.

"Well it's the dreams in general. Since I've been in this realm they seem different, like the fact you kissed me. And now this 'my love' stuff. I mean when the hell did that start happening?"

Jordan looked at her face and could see that she was determined to get an explanation. What could he tell her? That they were actually meeting up even though it was in dream form. No, she would want an explanation of how that was even possible and he couldn't tell her what he didn't know. Telling her that he had finally realised he loved her probably wouldn't go down to well either. She knew that they were meant to be together, Vincent had already told her that. Thinking of their last dream together he asked, "Has Vincent still got you chained up?"

"No, he has put me in my very own suite."

"Why would he do that?" Jordan asked not recalling reading anything about that in the book on her.

"I don't know," Charlotte replied shrugging. "Maybe he thinks being nice will make it easier for him to seduce me."

Jordan's jaw tightened at the sound of those last words. It still grated on his nerves. He also had to stop from asking if it would work. "So, what happened after our last dream?" he asked instead.

"Well I wasn't in the shackles Vincent had put me in anymore. They were lying next to my head as though someone had snuck in during the night and took them off me. I also sprained my ankle in an attempt to escape. Then would you believe, Vincent only chained me up again in a different place but standing up this time. He also knocked me out. The bastard."

"What?" said Jordan, he hoped he hadn't heard that correctly.

Charlotte looked at him with worry in her eyes. "He back handed me, really hard. It knocked me out."

"Why the hell would he hit you?" Anger and confusion welled up inside him. Then his confusion turned to rage. He remembered Vincent had back handed Sonya so hard it had sent her flying across the bedroom and smashing straight into the wall. He may despise the bitch, but he was glad no serious physical damage had been done to her. From that encounter, at least.

"I bit him and drew blood. It totally took him by surprise."

Is that pride he could hear in her voice?

"So, what happened next?" Jordan asked unable to hide the growl to his voice.

"I woke up in a comfortable bed and he has been very nice since then. He has nursed my sprained ankle for me and everything. Did you know he once had a soul mate?"

Jordan was rather shocked to hear that. The evil sadistic bastard he called uncle had once had a soul mate. Was she like him at all? Jordan couldn't help but wonder. He noticed the necklace on the bed by his pillow and he picked it up.

"What's that?" Charlotte asked him not seeing what he had.

"I got you a little something," he said bashfully. He held out the gift and showed her the heart shaped rose quartz necklace. He undid the clasp and leaned forward to put it around her neck. It only then occurred to him that he was having a dream and the necklace would be in his hands when he woke up.

"Thank you," she said as she tilted her head to the side. "Did you get this from my shop?"

"I see it and thought of you," he replied coyly.

"It's a very lovely gift. No matter where you got it from," she said. She smiled as she ran her fingers over the pendant.

Putting his hand under her chin Jordan turned Charlottes head to face him. Looking into her bright blue eyes which sparkled like gems Jordan slowly brought his head closer to her and not taking his eyes off hers he gently placed a kiss upon her lips.

"Time to wake up," was all he could say before she disappeared.

Chapter Twenty-Six

Charlotte slowly opened her eyes and felt like a giddy school girl again. Clearly the reaction was caused by Jordan's kiss. She lay there remembering the dream with a big goofy smile on her face. He had kissed her, again. Why did he keep doing that? Not that she was complaining, she loved the sensation of having his lips on hers. Considering it was something she had been wishing would happen since puberty was a bonus. When he called her 'My Love' and when he didn't answer her question hadn't escaped her notice either. It was a fact that she would have to bring up in another dream.

Feeling a slight weight on her chest Charlotte looked down. Her eyes widened in shock because there sat the rose quartz necklace Jordan had given her in the dream. She reached for the pendant and gently ran her fingers across it. Yep it was there, she wasn't imagining things.

"How in the hell?" she whispered. Was she still dreaming? How could it be there? So many different questions ran through her head at the same time. Something really strange was going on here but she didn't know why.

She shrugged it off for now and slowly sat herself up and grabbed the crutches. She slung her freshly washed clothes over her shoulder and headed for the bathroom. A short time later she emerged in her jeans a t-shirt and Jordan's jumper. She came to an abrupt stop when she spotted Vincent sitting on the chair by her bed.

"Good morning Charlotte, did you sleep well?" Vincent asked with a smile that revealed his straight white teeth.

"Morning, I did thanks."

Charlotte was taken off guard with him sitting there. He had such a dashing smile and mixed with the pleasantries she really didn't know what to make of his sudden personality change. What she did know was it put her on edge and her instincts were telling her not to believe any of it. Or was that her emotions calling her body a traitor? She wasn't quite sure. If she said that she didn't find Vincent attractive in any way she would be lying to herself. However, since he did have similarities to Jordan she chalked it up to that. It was still Jordan she wanted, always had been.

Vincent's sudden move to stand up brought her out of her thoughts.

"May I assist you to the breakfast table?" he asked as he walked over to her. He stopped and his gaze was drawn to the necklace. Lightly lifting the heart, he rested it on his fingers. "That's pretty. I don't recall you wearing it yesterday. Where did you get it from?" he asked and narrowed his eyes at her. Now, there was the Vincent she had come to know.

Charlotte looked at him and hoped her face didn't reveal the panic she felt coursing through her body. What was she going to say? What could she say 'Jordan gave it to me in my dream last night and I woke up with it on?' Yeah that would be believable. Not! Even though it was the truth. She was still trying to wrap her brain around how it had even been possible.

"It was in my pocket. I had forgotten I left it in the bathroom when I got changed yesterday." Jessica silently prayed that he believed the bull that had just come out of her gob.

Vincent eyed her suspiciously and debated if it was the truth or not. He had no proof either way so he decided to give her the benefit of the doubt for now. As he released the pendent from his fingers he watched as it fell back into place.

"Breakfast is served," he announced as he picked her up in his arms.

Chapter Twenty-Seven

Jordan woke with a smile on his face. He decided not to move just yet, so he lay there allowing his mind to go over his dream visit with Charlotte. Anger shot through him as he remembered that Vincent had struck her. She wasn't the first woman Vincent had struck either. Jordan had been present when Sonya had been smacked across a room, complements of one of his little rampages. Which made him wonder if Vincent had ever struck the woman who had been his soul mate?

Charlotte's words rang in his mind. She had told him 'he'd had a soul mate.' Jordan couldn't help but wonder who she was or where she was now. Had she died? Had he chased her away with his evil ways? Had he even been evil when he was with her? He just couldn't stop the barrage of thoughts bombarding his mind. Why did he care anyway? The man was a bastard, pure and simple.

He remembered the necklace he bought for Charlotte and checked himself to see if he still had it. Not being able to find it, he bolted out of the bed. He grabbed all the bed clothes individually and shook out each one before dropping them to the ground trying to find it. He couldn't stop the panic he felt running through his body.

"Where the hell is it?" he screeched looking at the bare mattress. All the bed clothes were lying in a heap on the floor next to him. He even went so far as to move the mattress to look under the bed. Wondering if someone had moved it he bolted for the kitchen.

"Has anyone seen the necklace I got for Charlotte?" Jordan asked in a panic. He entered the kitchen dining room area and almost fell over one of Jessica's dogs in the process.

"What?" said all three women at once, looking at Jordan as he made his way to the table.

"The necklace is gone," he said. He sat down and watched his grandmother's approach.

"Did you dream of Charlotte last night?" Christina asked placing a full English breakfast in front of him.

"Yes. Thank you," he replied for both the question and the breakfast.

"Did you give her the necklace in the dream?"

"Yes," he said tucking into his fried egg and fried bread. Finishing his mouth full he continued. "And now it's missing."

"Well that's where it is then. It's in Charlotte's possession."

"What?" The bit of bacon he had in his hand didn't quite get to its destination.

"Jordan darling," Christina started sitting opposite him at the table. "You have to remember that you are a descendant from Elves, Fae and Witches. I do not pretend to know everything about all the powers but you, unlike your father have more than just Elf powers."

"What's that got to do with the necklace being missing?"

"Well, Charlotte is a descendant from a supernatural being as well, although we don't know which one. Taking that into account and taking into account your highly unusual soul mate bond, I think you should just have faith that she has the necklace."

Jordan looked at his grandmother and didn't know how to reply to her have faith comment. Her previous statement did give him an idea though, if his mother wouldn't teach him to flash maybe his grandmother would. He glanced briefly at his mother who was busy with a book and felt it safe to continue.

"So, you're saying I should be able to flash and Dad can't?" Jordan knew Vincent had used that ability and knew how he had stolen that power.

"Yes exactly. It's not an Elf power. He has…well…basically a Jedi force stasis hold. You know like the one Darth Vader uses a lot." Christina knew her grandchildren were big Star Wars fans so she knew Jordan and Jessica would both know what she was getting at. "Hold up. What do you mean, should be able to flash? You can flash. My blood is in your veins as it is in your mothers."

"But I don't know how," he said putting on a little boy voice and pouting at his grandmother.

"Mother—" Isabella said trying to warn her.

"It's easy, you just concentrate on someone or somewhere and flash."

"Thanks Nan." Jordan smiled at his Nan and leant over the table and gave her a kiss on the cheek.

"Jordan Jason Elfin. You, crafty little fucker. That was out of order and you know it." Isabella said scolding her son.

"Isabella? What's the problem? He should already know how to use that ability."

"Well he didn't and under the current circumstances his father decided it best not to tell him."

"Why under the circumstances? …Oh." Realisation dawned on her. "Jordan when you flash it would drain your energy drastically because it isn't a dominant power of yours."

"I already told him that. Richard is going to go spare when he finds out about this."

"Where is Dad anyway?" Jordan asked only now noticing his Dad was nowhere to be found.

"He's gone to the other realm."

"WHAT?" Jordan screamed as he jumped out of his chair. He knocked the table in the process which sent tea spilling over the rims of all mugs.

"Sit down," Isabella's said in a stern voice. "Don't worry he hasn't gone to rescue Charlotte without you," she said noticing the look on his face.

"Why has he gone then?"

"You can change that tone right now young man," Isabella said giving him a look that said she was clearly not amused with him right now. A look she hadn't used in a while and thanks to Vincent. It probably wasn't as effective as it should have been now that she was technically the same age as her son. The glamour spell may have fooled her daughters and everyone else but Jordan knew the truth.

"He has gone to get some Intel on the situation."

"What?" Jordan said looking at his mother in confusion. Why was she trying to use military lingo?

"Oh, I don't know…He went to see what has been happening since Charlotte was taken. Trust me Jordan when it comes time for the rescue mission, you my son, will be leading the way."

Chapter Twenty-Eight

Richard stood in the middle of the war room. It still looked mostly the same as it always had. Grey stone walls were decorated with the colourful banners showing each General's crest. Most of them came from a long line of Elvin General's, with the odd exception. A lot had also changed in the last five years. Extra banners now adorned the walls, to signify new units. Much to his sister's delight the extra unit's all consisted of female Elves that she was in charge of.

The stained-glass windows showing various battle scenes hadn't changed, neither had the military tactical map table which still stood in the centre of the room. Looking at one of the battle scene window's it occurred to him that this room along with the main throne room were in fact the only rooms in the entire castle to have glass in the windows. Funny the things a person will think of when they have been away for a while.

When he took his gaze away from the windows he was greeted with the stares of his four top generals. Martouf, Lantash, Mattias and of course his sister. He couldn't help but notice how cosily she stood next to Lampros. If the rock on her finger was any indication, he knew why. How the hell had Lampros managed to finally nab his sister and when?

Being soul mates it was inevitable that they would end up together eventually but Trixie had been avoiding his advances for decades. So, he didn't know if he should be surprised or not. Richard knew he could trust Lampros with his life even if the Elf was his brother's best friend and his head general. But as far as loyalty went with Lampros he knew it was Trixie before anyone else and so did Vincent.

Richard also knew that Lampros walked a very fine line. It made it near impossible for him to not go against either Trixie or Vincent. But somehow, he managed to do just that. It was quite hard for him to watch Lampros kiss his sister passionately before he headed for the door.

"Where are you going?" he asked Lampros before he made it out of the room.

"I am going to keep myself busy your Majesty. I can't accidently tell Vincent something if I don't know about it," he said winking at Richard with a cheesy grin on his face before he left the room.

Richard turned to face his generals. They were all in their warrior uniforms except Mattias who didn't have one. As for his sister, she still looked like she had mugged Peter Pan and he currently looked more like an Elf version of James Dean.

After coming through to the Neutral Realm Richard had headed straight to the elfin castle war room. He hadn't bothered to go to his quarters and change so he imagined being in his elfin form which automatically changed upon his arrival and in his current attire he would look rather silly to some of the other Elves.

"Martouf," Richard said addressing his head general. "Do we have any information?"

"We know that Vincent has the girl. Exactly where and in what castle we have been unable to find out," Martouf said. "My lord why is Prince Jordan not present for this meeting?"

"It turns out the girl, as you put it, is Jordan's soul mate. Since the call of the rose hasn't started I decided to leave him back in the Human Realm. Not only would his presence here be a distraction for everyone else but he would also no doubt go off half-cocked on his own to get Charlotte back. That I cannot have. So, while her life is in no immediate danger he stays put. Plus, he still has a sister to go and visit," he said with a smirk.

"What's the significance of that?" Lantash asked cocking an eyebrow.

"My daughters are just like their Auntie Trixie," he replied as he looked at his sister who was giving him a dirty look.

"Say no more your Majesty," Martouf replied glancing at Trixie. He had known her all her life and knew how feisty she could sometimes be. "Let's just hope your son makes it back from his visit in one piece."

Laughter washed over the room at the fiery look on Trixie's face. A move Martouf had made on purpose to lighten the mood and he also loved to wind her up. He walked up to her and put his arm around her shoulders. He looked down at her with his gleaming blue eyes "You know I love you, right?" he jested. It was a comment that earned him an elbow in the gut.

"Will Princess Jessica be coming through as well? I know she is due to go to the Realm of the Fae soon but isn't it her best friend that Vincent had taken?" Lantash asked.

"Princess Jessica is currently getting a crash course from Christina on how to use her powers. Yes Lantash, she will also be accompanying us through to this realm," he said as he placed a finger to his lips in thought.

"Actually, thinking about it, she might benefit from all your expertise. After this meeting is finished and you have your orders, we will reconvene in a week if not sooner. In this time, you three can give her a crash course in weapons," Richard looked at each of his generals in turn. "Now back to the business at hand."

Looking towards Trixie, Richard continued. "Where did you go?"

"When?" she asked him.

"When Jordan came through to the other realm he said you were doing recon."

"I went to see Lampros."

"Why?" Richard asked cocking his eyebrow.

"To see what he knew."

"Tracey, you can't do that," Richard said sternly narrowing his eyes at his sister.

"That's what he said," she replied noticing her brother's tone and the use of her actual name. "Don't worry it won't happen again."

"It had better not. He is in a difficult enough position as it is and he doesn't need you making it worse for him."

Dragging his attention back to the tactical map he surveyed all the area's that were a part of the Elvin realm. He concentrated on the section from the main castle to the Autumn Elves Castle. Since that was Vincent's main place of residence. Thinking back to when they were children Richard thought their father should have given Vincent the Winter Palace. The elves there were cold and cruel, just like him. He would have felt right at home and they may have even kept him from causing the problems he was now.

"Our main problem will be getting into the Autumn Castle. I don't know about you but I would really like to avoid what happened last time," Richard looked at each Elf in turn. "We need to find out exactly where in the castle Vincent is keeping Charlotte."

"How do you know that Vincent is holding her in the Autumn Elves Castle?" Martouf asked. "We haven't been able to find out anything of importance and we have been here?"

Richard eyed Martouf carefully. It had been a fair question and if they were going to get Charlotte back with minimum casualties they did need to know everything. It wasn't like he didn't trust any of those present. He had been with Martouf, Lantash and Mattias since they were all young Elf-lings. "We have two advantages in our favour. The first one being that Jordan and Charlotte share dreams."

"What? How is that even possible?"

It was Trixie that asked and she looked clearly shocked by the news. Everyone in the room was looking at him as Trixie was, which told Richard what they were all thinking.

"We don't know yet unfortunately. We are working that out right now but this is still an advantage. There are also The Book of the Realms, one of which is on Charlotte herself. We don't know exactly know why she has a book yet either. But we are working on it," Richard finished looking at his sister.

"Well. That's a confusing bonus I think," Trixie said.

"Right," Richard said clapping his hands. "I'm going to head back to the Human Realm before my son starts having kittens at me for being here for so long. Martouf take a group of elves and find out how many guards Vincent has around his castle. Find any weaknesses we may be able to exploit. Don't forget the secret passages because they connect to all the castles," said Richard. Martouf came to attention nodded his head towards Richard and left the room. Richard them moved his attention to his next general.

"Lantash, I want you to check out the dark forest in the direction of the Autumn Castle and surrounding it. I know my brother he will have it guarded. He knows Charlotte's importance and that we will be coming for her. Something tells me that he won't give her up without a fight." Lantash came to attention and with a nod of his head he also headed out the door.

Richard turned his attention to Mattias who was standing there casually leaning up against the wall. He was in a different league to Martouf and Lantash. He was wearing skin tight black leather trousers and a black wrap around shirt that moulded to his form. It highlighted his impressive physique and left nothing to the imagination. He stood to attention and gave a slight bow to his king. "Your Majesty."

"Mattias, you do what you do best," was all Richard needed to say. Mattias had skills and abilities the elves did not.

"Your Majesty," Mattias said before bowing his head and leaving the room. He gave Trixie a curt nod as he walked past her.

"What does he do best?" Trixie asked her brother as she watched Mattias leave the room enjoying the scrumptious eye-candy's retreat.

"Tracey Elizabeth."

"What?" Trixie asked. She was upset that her brother had now used her middle name as well. "I can perve can't I?"

"You sound just like Jessica and Charlotte," Richard replied rubbing his right temple with his index and middle fingers. "I'm going to head back to the other realm. Jordan may have something to tell us from his subconscious visits with Charlotte."

"Wait…. what do you want me to do?" Trixie asked noticing he hadn't given her any orders.

He walked over to his sister and placed his hands on either side of her shoulders. "You do what you do best," he smiled and gave her a kiss on top of her head.

As they headed to the door Richard suddenly stopped dead making Trixie bump into him.

"What is it?" she asked concerned at the worried look on his face.

"Something's wrong. Jordan's in the Realm."

"He couldn't have got here that fast. It would be impossible."

"Not if someone had told him how to flash," he said in frustration. "Damn it."

"What can we do?" Trixie said with worry.

"We can't do a fucking thing," said Richard as he felt a familiar humming course through his body. "Fucking great, now 'the call' has been activated. I'm going to fucking kill him myself."

Richard stormed out the door like his arse was on fire and Trixie tried to catch up.

"MATTIAS."

Within seconds Mattias flashed in front of Richard who was so angry with his son he didn't even flinch, like he would normally do.

"Richard?"

"Go and get Jordan," Richard ordered.

"My Lord?" Mattias said with confusion.

"Go and get my son, damn it. NOW."

"Bollocks." Mattias felt the humming of the call just seconds before he flashed. He returned a mere seconds later with Jordan in his arms.

"Oh, my god," Trixie yelped as she covered her mouth with her hands.

Richard cast her a quick glance before kneeling beside his son. He checked to make sure he was still alive. Jordan groaned slightly when Richard brushed his hand over his left shoulder. Richard couldn't believe he hadn't noticed the blast burn on his son.

"What the fuck happened?" Richard looked at Mattias who was still on his knees from placing Jordan on the floor.

"I'd say Vincent shot him."

"What the fuck?" Richard went to get up but Mattias stopped him with a hand to his shoulder.

"I think it was an instant reaction. Jordan's sudden arrival would have startled him. However, I did get there before your brother could finish the job."

"Thank you," Richard said clasping Mattias on the shoulder. He slowly released the breath he hadn't realised he'd be holding. "What's wrong with your ear?"

"Hysterical females, you've gotta love them," he answered as he wiggled his finger in his ear to try and stop the ringing.

Trixie stepped forward to observe the scene.

"I don't understand. A power bolt shot wouldn't have knocked him out and he's part Fae so nor would him flashing."

"It would if he'd flashed from the Human Realm," Richard stated flatly.

"Jordan wouldn't have been that stupid. Surely."

"Clearly, he was damn it. Damn it. Damn it." Richard cursed.

"Richard that is enough," scolded Trixie glaring at her brother. "Now you are going to pull yourself together. Do you hear me?"

"I'm good," he said taking in a deep breath. He glanced at his sister before picking up his son and slinging him over his shoulder in a fireman's lift. God, he weighted a tonne. "Mattias, would you be alright to flash us back to the Human Realm. I have a feeling Isabella has no idea whatsoever that Jordan's left the house."

"Sure, no sweat," he said on a shrug.

"Trixie, I will see you soon."

Trixie didn't get a chance to answer him before he flashed straight to the kitchen of Rose Manor.

"Who the fuck told him how to flash?" Richard bellowed making everyone jump in the process. He didn't actually expect to get an answer. Not once they saw what he carried over his shoulder.

"Jordan," Isabella screeched and rushed over to inspect her son. "What the hell happened?"

"That would be my question," he said adjusting his son on his shoulder. "I thought he was going to see Janice."

"We thought he was upstairs getting ready." The look on Isabella's face was enough to break Richard's heart.

"Hold that thought, he's a heavy bastard."

Richard left the room and returned without his son draped over his shoulder. Glancing over the kitchen he realised that nobody had moved an inch. He walked to the fridge and grabbed two beers, handing one to Mattias. He opened the other for himself and took a very long swig. Mattias nodded and continued to play with his ear.

Isabella stood by the kitchen table with her arms folded over her chest and her eyebrows raised. She was clearly waiting for one of the two elves to answer her original question. Her impatience was evident when her fingers started tapping for forearms.

"Don't you give me that look," Richard said as he pointed at his wife. He'd be damned if he was about to be the one in trouble for his son's idiotic actions.

"And what look is that?" Isabella was just as defiant.

"The look that says you want answers. Well you know what? So, the hell do I, now who the hell told our son how to flash?" Richard was trying desperately not to have a yelling match with his wife but he could see it coming.

"It doesn't matter who told him."

"I'm going to—" Christina said as she started to rise from her chair.

"You're fucking staying put," Richard ordered not taking his eyes off his wife. His mother-in-law slowly sank back into her seat. "So, your mother is the one who told him."

"Our son tricked her into giving him the information he should already have known."

"And what has that done?"

"You tell me."

"NEARLY GOTTEN HIM KILLED," Richard bellowed. "If it wasn't for Mattias being able to flash better than the fucking Fae can our son would be dead now. Killed by my fucking brother and for what? His impatience over a fucking woman."

Isabella gasped at her husband stunned by his reaction. She didn't know what had stunned her more, what could have happened to Jordan or how he had referred to Charlotte. She had also never seen him this angry in the thirty-five years they had been together. Not even when Vincent had tried to seduce her had Richard been this mad. What happened to Jordan must have really scared him?

"Richard I—"

"I'm going to the fucking pub," he said slamming his empty bottle into the sink. He turned and headed for the door. "Mattias, come on."

Isabella just stood there watching her husband storm out of the house with Mattias in tow. What else could she do?

Smirking to herself she yelled at the top of her lungs.

"JORDAN, GET YOUR FUCKING ARSE UP."

Chapter Twenty-Nine

A few hours later Richard stood with his arms folded and was leaning up against the closed half of the double glass doors leading to the garden. He was still fuming at Jordan over his earlier stunt but there was little he could do about it now. He wasn't even home yet and Isabella had already laid into him for it. It was something they had always done. If Isabella had told the kids off for something, then he would let it slide. He had never told them off for the same thing and he wasn't about to start now. Even if he did want to inform his son how stupid he had been.

He watched his daughter firing bolts of light at a makeshift target he had no doubt Christina put together. He had been glad when Mattias had gone back to the Elvin Realm. Not because he was glad to get rid of his general but because Mattias and Jessica had been a little too cosy for his liking. Even if they hadn't noticed it.

Richard felt a hand running up his back and he turned to see Isabella standing next to him. He smiled at her as he placed a kiss on her lips and turned back to observe their daughter.

"Penny for your thought," Isabella said as she looked up at her husband. She could see by the look in his eyes he was thinking.

Turning his head and looking down into her eyes he answered, "Which one?"

"The one that is screaming at you the loudest," she replied with a smile.

"The upcoming battle," Richard replied feeling overwhelmed by it all.

"You really think it will come to that?" she asked with apprehension.

Richard raised his eyebrow at her. He knew that Vincent would deliberately make it hard for them to get Charlotte back. No amount of planning could prevent any blood-shed to come. Vincent could still be the crack that would make the walls come tumbling down. With one word, he answered her question.

"Yes."

"How can you be so sure?"

"Vincent really wants to hurt our son. If not through death, then by other means so having Charlotte works to his benefit. The longer he has her the more time he has to seduce her which just adds to the mental torture that Jordan would be going through. He's not going to be able to stop the images of Vincent and Charlotte together from popping into his head."

"And if Vincent succeeds in seducing her?"

"That is something we must prepare for. Jordan has only recently realised his feelings for Charlotte and with their bond being unusually strong, something like that could break him. A broken Prince cannot rule a realm so either way Vincent wins."

"Well it's a good thing I'm coming too."

"What? Oh, no you're not," Richard said sternly.

"Excuse me?" Isabella said raising her eyebrows at him and placing her hands on her hips.

"You're not going. It will be bad enough that Jordan and Jessica will be there."

"And you seriously think I am going to sit here all safe and sound while my husband, son and daughter are risking their lives. I don't think so mister," she glared at him in defiance. "You know I have my own powers so it's not like I'm going to be defenceless."

"You are not going and that is final."

"Who the hell do you think you're talking to like that?"

"Isabella," Richard sighed. He had to tell her.

"No, I am not one of the kids, you can just—"

"You're pregnant."

"I'M WHAT?"

"Pregnant."

"Bullshit. I can't believe you would stoop so low as to say something like that."

"Check the family tree," he said nodding in the direction of the table.

"Check the tree, check the tree. I'll check the fucking tree," she fumed rummaging through the books and paper work on the table until she found what she was looking for. "You've got to be shitting me."

The stunned look on her face put a smirk on his. "Perhaps we should have been more careful other night."

"That's not funny," she said rolling the tree back up. "This changes nothing."

"What? Isabella, you can't."

"Isabella can and Isabella will and you my husband can't stop me. You do not have the power too. If you don't take me with you, I will turn up any way."

"Fine." There was clearly no talking her out of it if not even being pregnant was deterring her. She had a point and he had no way of stopping her. "But, I'm not happy about this."

"And I aint bov-vered," she replied in a very thick London accent as she walked off.

Richard watched his wife's retreat. Damn that TV show, he thought as his attention was drawn back to Jessica and her training. He smiled at the look on his daughter's face. She was clearly enjoying herself as she flashed all over the garden. Knowing how much of a Star Wars fan she was he wondered how she would react when she found out she could do the thing that Vader does as Christina had put it.

Chapter Thirty

Jessica flashed in right behind her dad and couldn't help but crack up laughing when he jumped and dropped his coffee cup which smashed on the ground.

"That's not funny young lady," Richard said. Isabella passed him the dust pan and brush while scowling at her daughter. She'd only just made that. "Here. You're cleaning up that mess since you caused it," he said as he held out the dustpan and brush for her.

"Well that's crap," Jessica said as she grabbed the items her father handed to her and started to clean up the mess.

"That will teach you to use your powers wisely, every action has a consequence," Richard replied, smirking at the scowl on her face.

The front door slammed and drew Richards's attention in that direction. He turned and found his son standing there with a black eye. "What the hell happened to you?"

"I got into a fight," Jordan replied. His mother came rushing over to check his injured shoulder from earlier. "Mum I'm okay. Will you stop fussing please," he said playfully smacking her hands away from him.

"What is it with you today?" Isabella asked. "What happened this time? You only went to see your sister."

"Speaking of my sister, is there something you guys forgot to mention?"

"Like what?" Isabella asked, frowning.

"I don't know," Jordan said shrugging. "Like the fact, she is married. And when was I going to be told I am an uncle?"

"I'm sure we told…" said Isabella with uncertainty.

"No, you didn't and it turns out that her husband - Whatever the hell his name is—"

"Scott," Jessica said helpfully.

"Yeah him." Jordan said pointing at his sister before looking back at his mother. "Is a possessive insecure prick. All I was doing was hugging my little sister and this ponce grabs my injured shoulder -I might add - dragging me away from my sister and slugged me one."

"And you automatically fought back," Isabella added.

"Your damn right I did. Oh, you might want to give Janice a call," Jordan said.

"Why?"

"She might be a little upset."

"What else happened?" Isabella groaned.

"She kind of told him she was sick of his jealousy and punching me was the last straw. She told him to stick it," he said with a nod.

"Bloody kids," Isabella muttered as she went into the living room to call her daughter.

Jordan turned to his father once his mother was out of site.

"So, what did you find out?"

"Before or after you almost got yourself killed?" Richard replied folding his arms.

"Dad—"

"I don't want to hear it. If you ever go against my orders again I will have your grandfather strip you of your powers. I don't care if you are my son you will then spend the next month in a dungeon cell for insubordination. Do I make myself clear?"

"Yes father."

"Good."

Richard waited for Isabella to come back, when she and everyone else had returned and taken their seats he continued.

"It would seem the book on Charlotte has come in very handy. Martouf hasn't been able to find out where Charlotte is being kept. But it is definitely a big advantage for us and we are going to have to keep a close eye on it for any changes."

"So, what happens now?" Jordan asked not being able to hide the aggravation in his voice. This couldn't be all that they were doing.

"Well providing The Call of the Rose hasn't been set off for her. We go through in a week."

"A week.... Are you kidding me??" Jordan was so overcome with anger he had to clench his fists to avoid punching something. He was still pissed off from his argument earlier and the fact his mother and grandmother had been right.

Richard stood to his full height and folded his arms over his chest cocking one eyebrow at his son. "Are you quite finished?"

"Yes," Jordan replied through gritted teeth.

Richard was starting to lose even more patience with his son's behaviour. "Right. We go through in a week. That will give Martouf, Lantash and Mattias time to complete their assigned missions."

"What missions?" Jordan asked curiously.

"Does it matter?" Richard asked in frustration.

"I think it does," Jordan replied.

"Martouf is checking out the castles, Lantash is checking out the forests...."

"What's Mattias doing?"

"If you hadn't interrupted me, I would have gotten to that. He is finding out exactly where Charlotte is being held in the castle. After that stunt you pulled today Vincent may have already moved her."

"Why him?" Jordan asked with worry.

Richard just stood there. He knew the reputation Mattias had with females of any species, he wasn't fussy. Which gave him more reason for concern especially where his daughter was concerned.

"Because he is good at what he does."

"Yeah I know what he's good at. Why couldn't you have sent Lantash or Martouf instead?" Jordan glanced briefly at the book on Charlotte. "Yeah, Martouf would have been the better one to send."

Richard couldn't believe what was coming out of his son's mouth. "What's the matter son you afraid of a bit of competition?" Richard teased knowing it would really get his son riled up.

"What competition? Charlotte loves me," Jordan said sounding rather smug. "Ouch, what the hell?" Jordan said turning around in his chair. His mother had just slapped him across the back of the head.

"It has only been a few days since you realised that you felt the same. So, you can stop acting like a jealous teenager and god's gift to women. I raised you better than that," snapped Isabella.

"Yes Mum," he answered feeling like the teenager she was referring to. Looking at his father he continued. "So, what happens when we go through?"

"Jessica is getting a crash course in weapons from Martouf, Lantash and Mattias."

"Do you think that is wise?" Jordan asked just before getting another clip around the back of his head from his mother. He turned his head to look at her. "What? I'm thinking of my sister this time. I've been around those elves. I know what they are like."

Richard started rubbing his temples, feeling like he was getting a migraine. "Jessica will be perfectly safe. Martouf is with his soul mate and as for Lantash and Mattias they will not touch her knowing she's my daughter. So, unless one of them turns out to be her soul mate you can stop worrying about your sister's virtue."

Jessica cut a look at her brother and had an uncontrollable urge to smack him. She fought it as she turned to her dad. "Won't I be stuck there once I go through?"

"Technically yes. However, due to the current circumstances and why you are going through early we will petition the elders to allow you time back in the human realm to get your affairs in order," he replied smiling at his daughter.

"Do you think they will let me back through?"

"I don't know, but I think we will have at least six votes in our favour," he replied cutting a look at his mother-in-law. "Do you agree Christina?"

"You're a sly old fox, however I have to agree." She smiled knowing exactly who on the council of elders he was referring too.

"Speaking of the elders, have you heard back from Tristan yet?"

"Did somebody say my name?" Tristan said as he walked into the kitchen.

Unlike Richard and Christina his appearance didn't change when he came to the Human Realm. Standing there in a black suit and a crisp white shirt and a clichéd cape was Tristan. He ran his eyes over everyone in the room and when he spotted the look on Jessica's face, he held out his arms to her.

"Hello Darling," he said smiling.

"Grand-dad." Jessica said running into his arms and hugging him as tightly as she could.

Chapter Thirty-One

"What did the elders say?" Richard asked Tristan once he was seated.

"Honestly?" said Tristan sternly. Richard nodded as he took a seat opposite his father-in-law. "The elders are in the dark as much as we are."

"What? How is that even possible?" Richard didn't like the sound of that.

"I don't know. What I do know is that they are aware of the soul mate bond between Jordan and Charlotte and are fully aware of both of their heritages."

"Both their heritages?" Richard said raising his eyebrow at Tristan.

"Yes, turns out Charlotte does in fact have supernatural blood running through her veins."

"What species?"

"Witch, and possibly a second one. They aren't one hundred percent sure on that bit."

"Charlotte is part witch?" Isabella asked.

"It would seem so. However, none of the elders know why the bond between Jordan and Charlotte is so strong. The strongest they have ever seen in fact."

"Surely someone knows something?" Christina said.

"I imagine someone would especially if they had been around before the Realms were conceived," Tristan replied.

"Loki," Isabella whispered. Blushing.

"Who?" Tristan asked.

"Loki," Isabella said a little louder. "He's older than dirt, so wouldn't he know?"

"Who's Loki?" Jessica asked.

"He is a very old shifter," Christina said with a smile. "Your mother's first crush."

"Really?" Jessica asked.

"Yes. You know the effect your brother has on all of your girl friends?" Christina said and Jessica nodded. "Well. Loki has the same effect."

Richard rolled his eyes. The last thing he needed was his daughter going goo-goo-eyed over the man. He decided to change the subject so he cleared his throat. "Getting back to the matter at hand. Would Loki know?"

"Possibly. However, he's currently in America maintaining Daffodil Manor and is unreachable," Christina answered.

"So, where the hell does that leave us?" Richard asked in frustration.

"To expect, the unexpected I guess," Tristan replied. "With the elders not knowing what's going on anything is possible."

"Isn't there an oracle or something we can consult?" Richard asked running his fingers through his hair.

"Richard, this is not ancient Greece. There are no oracles and there hasn't been a known seer among the witches in centuries. If there are any, they're not making themselves known. Foresight unfortunately isn't a power my line has been blessed with," Tristan said.

"Well what about Ruby's line?" Richard asked in desperation. He didn't like the feeling of not being in control. If the elders didn't know what was going on, Richard shuddered at the thought. He had enough to deal with where his brother was concerned, never mind anything else.

"Nor does her line," Tristan answered before turning to Jordan. "How are you feeling?"

Jordan just looked at his grandfather in confusion.

Tristan stared at him waiting for an answer. "Well…How do you feel right now?"

"Fine I guess…why?" Jordan asked still confused.

"Now concentrate on Charlotte and tell me how you feel?"

"Ok," Jordan replied even more confused.

Closing his eyes Jordan focused on nothing but Charlotte. A feeling of calm came over him. He opened his eyes and looked at his grandfather.

"I feel calm and peaceful. What would that mean?"

Tristan turned his gaze to Richard who just nodded. They both knew what that meant.

He turned to Christina. "They meet up in their dreams?" she nodded her assent. "And what happens in the dreams manifests in the waking world or vice versa?"

"It would seem so. But we only have the necklace Jordan gave to her in their dream to go on," Christina replied.

Tristan glanced at everyone in the room, before staring intently at Jordan. Reaching into his pocket he pulled out a small pouch. Untying the leather binding he grabbed a handful of the contents.

"Do whatever it is you both feel compelled to do," he said ignoring the frown of confusion on Jordan's face.

"Sorry Isabella," Tristan said glancing at his daughter.

"For what?" Isabella got nervous at her father's words and started rising from her seat.

"For what I'm about to do." Opening his palm, he blew the fine golden powder that rested there into his grandson's face.

Jordan blinked a few times when the powder hit his face. Without any warning, Jordan's eyes rolled back and his head hit the table.

"What the hell have you done?" Isabella screeched at her father as she ran over to her son's side, worry etched in the lines of her face. "If you have hurt my son."

"You'll do what?" Tristan asked as he stood from the chair. Everyone else seemed to be in too much of a momentary daze at his unexpected action to react.

"I'll use my Fae powers on you," she sneered through gritted teeth.

"All I have done is send him to Charlotte," Tristan replied. He ignored the daggered look his daughter was throwing at him.

"What the hell for?" Isabella asked in anger.

"I have my reasons," he said adjusting his cape before he strode out of the room.

Chapter Thirty-Two

Jordan opened his eyes and sat up he grabbed his head as pain shot through it. He felt like he had the biggest hang over ever. What had his grandfather done to him? He looked over his surroundings and couldn't miss Charlotte leaning against the door frame. She was swinging the belt from the robe she was wearing. Jordan couldn't help notice how see-through the material was or how little it hid what lay beneath. He looked her over with hungry eyes and swallowed down his emotions.

"I've been expecting you," Charlotte drawled as she slowly walked across the room towards him still spinning the belt of her robe. Her eyes gleamed in the light and were filled with a red-hot passion he had never seen in her before. Was she under some kind of spell? Did she even know who she was talking to or did she think he was Vincent? Did he succeed in seducing her? A thousand different questions consumed his mind especially when he realised they were in Vincent's boudoir. He had to be dreaming this or by some twist of fate he had somehow been thrown into Vincent's body while he was seducing Charlotte. No that couldn't be right. His grandfather would never be as cruel as to do something like that, would he? Jordan wasn't sure of anything anymore.

Charlotte stopping in front of him brought him out of his thoughts. He was laying down but couldn't help taking a long lingering look at her from her feet all the way up to her head. He couldn't help but hover over certain areas a little longer than others. She was exquisite. He tried shaking his head to regain some of his focus but winced as pain pulsed through his skull. He looked up at her and felt the desire to touch her pulse even stronger through his body. He felt the muscles of his manhood twitch with need at the sight of her delicious curves.

What the hell was going on? He shifted his body to get off the bed but was stopped dead in his tracks as she placed her hand on his shoulder and pushed him back down against the pillows.

"Charlotte?"

"Shush my love."

Placing her knee on the bed she swung her other leg over his torso, straddling him. He couldn't help the desire that rippled through his body. She looked damn sexy he almost couldn't contain himself. Did he even want to? He was suddenly drawn from his thoughts when her long blonde hair caressed his face and before he had time to think of anything else her lips were on his and her tongue was demanding access to his mouth. All Jordan could do was acquiesce to her demands. He showed her all the emotions she stirred within him as their tongues battled for dominance. He wanted to taste her, he wanted to feel her surrounding him and he wanted to breathe her in and never let go.

He was powerless to stop what he was feeling. They devoured each other's mouths like they had been starving all this time. Jordan placed his palms on her face holding her to him so it never had to end. He kissed her with every ounce of passion he felt within him but even with passion coursing through his veins he couldn't shake the feeling that something wasn't right. He still wasn't sure if she even knew who he was. The passionate groan he heard from her mouth sent shivers of desire coursing through his body. He needed to know if she knew it was him and what she was doing to him.

He gently broke the kiss and retreated just enough to look up into her eyes. All he could see was passion clouding her vision. She wasn't the innocent Charlotte he had known most of his life, nor the young woman he had watched grow up and without knowing it, fallen deeply in love with.

Before him was a woman who had only one thing on her mind. She was a temptress and his body was responding to hers in every way. This felt wrong to him somehow. His sweet and innocent Charlotte had become a seductress and was determined to have her wicked way with him. As much as that thought sent pleasurable shivers coursing through him there was only one thought racing through his head at that moment.

"Who am I?"

Charlotte looked at him in confusion at first but gradually that melted away with the rising heat of the moment.

"My lover," she replied bringing her head down towards his jaw and placing a kiss just under his ear. "My heart's desire," she said kissing him again. "My soul mate," she said as she began to place feather kisses along his neck. Jordan swallowed hard at the feelings she was provoking within him. He wondered if she

was going to continue kissing him as he asked her questions. Not that he was going to complain.

He closed his eyes and tilted his head slightly to give her better access to his throat. He placed his hands on her thighs and enjoyed the sensations that rippled through his body every time her lips touched his skin.

He felt Charlotte's hands cup his jaw and her lips brush lightly over his and when he opened his eyes he was met with hers. Her beautiful emerald green eyes - Green? He was sure her eyes were blue - Either way, no longer were they filled with sexual hunger, love was all he saw now. He was mesmerised by their beauty and so caught up in her gaze he almost missed her words.

"Make love to me Jordan."

Those five simple words sent a multitude of emotions crashing into him. He was well and truly done for.

Dream or not the passion that she had stirred within him spread like a wild fire. He would be severely pissed off if he was to wake up now. Jordan finally succumbed to the emotions he was feeling and grabbed the back of Charlottes head. With a fist-full of her blonde locks he lifted her head and crushed his mouth to hers. Her moans of pleasure only added fuel to the already smouldering fire within him, spurring him on. He couldn't recall a time when he had hungered for a woman as much as he did now, he wanted to stay in this moment forever.

He could feel her hands running up and down his back and her nails digging into his flesh with every stroke of his tongue. It was only then did he realise he was only clothed in pants and they were suddenly feeling uncomfortably tight. When had she undressed him? Was he even wearing a shirt when this bizarre dream started, he didn't know. All he knew was he didn't want to leave. Trying to concentrate on anything more than what was happening between him and Charlotte was impossible.

Jordan ventured from her lips slowly placing kisses across her jaw and down her neck, tasting her skin with each kiss. The sounds she made encouraged him to continue his path. He placed small kisses along her neck line down to the opening in her robe. He slowly pulled the material off her shoulders so it fell to her waist revealing her amazing breasts in all their glory. Desire, want and need filled his body until he thought he was going to lose control over his own body. How could one woman have such a powerful effect on him? Had she always had that effect?

Jordan laid her down on the bed and untied the belt of the robe revealing the beauty beneath it. He gently ran his finger tip over the contours of her body and heat flowed to his groin as he watched her arch her back and groan with pleasure.

Taking full advantage of her position he lowered his head over her left breast and took her nipple into his mouth. He slowly started sucking and licking her flesh feeling the nipple harden from his touch. He felt her body shudder as he gently swiped his teeth over the hardened peak. He wanted nothing more in that moment than to take her in all her glory. He wanted to hear her moans of pleasure as his hardness filled her completely.

He sat up in between her thighs and the dampness he felt on his pants told him how much she wanted him. He cupped her breasts in each hand and caressed them slowly rubbing his thumbs over each nipple. He could see the need in her face and saw more than that when she opened her eyes and looked at him. He could feel the heat from her body as she ran her finger tips over his torso and down his abs to his waste. He closed his eyes and rolled his head back allowing the pleasure of her touch to wash over him feeding the hunger he felt for her.

Jordan felt Charlotte stirring in the bed. She sat up to get a better grip on his pants and he opened his eyes and looked into hers. They were filled with so much passion he swallowed hard at the sight of them. He grabbed the nape of her neck and lowered his head down to her and took her lips in a fiery kiss. He lifted his hips and allowed her to remove his pants freeing his throbbing erection. Her hand gripped his long shaft tightly and sent shivers through his body. He was surprised he didn't spill his load then and there. Jordan removed her hand from his thick shaft and slowly slid off the bed, smiling at Charlotte when she pouted at him. Jordan knelt on the floor next to the bed and grabbed her ankles sliding her easily to the edge of the bed and placing her legs over his shoulders.

Kissing along her thigh he made his way to the neat curls of her centre. He ran his tongue from her opening to her clit and swirled the tip of his tongue over her swollen nub. He moved down and speared his tongue into her moist centre, her taste was ambrosia to his senses. Her deep moans made him even hungrier for her essence and he licked her harder and faster making her squirm on the bed underneath him.

"Jordan. I need you inside me," she gasped.

Stopping what he was doing he gazed over her body to her pleasure induced features.

"Patience, my love."

"Why, I need you. Can't you just whack it in there?"

"No," Jordan said raising his eyebrows at her comment. He had never had a woman say that to him.

"Why not?" she said with a hint of frustration in her voice.

"I need to make sure you are ready for me. Otherwise it will hurt like hell," he said and smiled at the pout of her lips. "Did you learn nothing from reading all those romances?"

She sat up slightly and rested with her arms behind her slightly.

"You're not going to tell me how tight I am, are you?" she said narrowing her eyes at him.

"No, of course not," he said. He was sure he had said that once or twice over the years. "Even though you would be because you are untouched, pure." He smiled at the shocked looked on her face. "Why would you ask that?"

"I hate it when the blokes in the book say it."

"You won't hear me say it then."

"Good," she said and laid back down on the sheets. Her eyes drifted down her body so she could watch him.

"Move up the bed a bit," Jordan asked her as he stood up. His penis hit his stomach as he watched her inch up the bed, he didn't think it could get any harder.

When she complied, he placed himself between her thighs and his cock nudged at the lips of her centre. He grabbed his thick shaft and placed it at her opening, his slight hesitation gave her pause.

"What is it?" she asked with worry.

"If we were in the waking world, I would have a condom on already."

"What for?"

"So, you didn't fall pregnant." Her mischievous grin made him nervous for a second.

"Jordan this is a dream. I may have dreamt that I was carrying your child and wished with all my heart and soul that it would one day happen but I'm pretty sure tonight will not be that night. As much as I may wish it was." She leaned up and placed a kiss to his lips.

A cold shiver ran through him at her words but he shrugged it off and eased into her. Her back arched as he slowly sank into her moist centre. Her walls gripped him like a vice, so tightly he was surprised his eyes hadn't bulged out of his head. Jordan stopped half way into her welcoming heat and noticed she was biting her bottom lip. She looked so sexy that way and he took a moment to commit it to memory. He was brought back to reality when she started wiggling her bum trying to get comfortable.

He couldn't begin to imagine the discomfort she was feeling which only added to his, knowing that it was him causing it. Pain shot through his already painful cock at it was jarred from side to side and he couldn't help but grit his teeth.

"Will you stop wiggling your arse or I will tell you exactly how tight you are."

Charlotte stopped instantly and Jordan rested on his elbow on the bed and brushed the hair from her face.

"Just relax and let your body adjust," he said giving her a reassuring smile and placing a kiss to her lips, which she returned in kind. Jordan was so distracted by the kiss that he didn't even realise that he was inside her to the hilt. The only indication from Charlotte were her nails digging into his back. Her grip was so hard he was sure she had broken the skin, in fact, he was positive of it. He felt the familiar stinging sensation that trailed after her nails along his back. Jordan withdrew slightly and slowly plunged back in, he froze when he heard her gasp.

"Are you alright?" he said with concern. He was scared he had hurt her.

"Yes, I'm fine," she said as she wrapped her legs around his hips and locked her ankles together.

He breathed out slowly with relief at her words. He lifted her and moved them further up the bed before gently laying her back down. Withdrawing from her slowly he kissed a long her collar and thrust back into her welcoming warmth.

Jordan entwined their fingers together and placed them above her head. He gradually set a steady pace with each of his thrusts and found himself luxuriating in the depths and sweetness of her beautiful body. The sweat glistened on their skin as they came together on each thrust. Never had something felt so right to him and never had he wanted to please anyone more than he wanted to please Charlotte in this moment.

The way she was breathing told Jordan she was close to climax. With each pleasure filled moan of his name his control slipped a little further. It was taking him everything he had not to pound into her glorious body. He felt his balls tighten and her muscles grip him like a vice until her whole body shattered around him as she reached her climax. Her satisfied screams were music to his ears. Jordan stroked long and deep into Charlottes core wanting to feel every part of her release. He could feel the familiar tingling in his spine that signified the beginning of his own release so he pushed into her even further until his release washed over him and he spilt his seed deep within her.

He rested on his forearms so not to crush her and grabbed her around the waist, rolling them so she was lying on him. The top of her head lay just under his chin and he could feel her breathing become shallow. She placed a light kiss to his chest before resting her head there once again. He could tell the moment she had fallen into a peaceful slumber.

"I love you," he whispered and placed a kiss on her head then he too fell into a peaceful slumber.

Chapter Thirty-Three

Isabella sat at the kitchen table on her own. After what her father had done and when he left everyone else seemed to have dispersed from the room shortly after. Her mother and daughter had taken the dogs for a walk and Richard had taken Jordan up to his room. He was now in the lounge-room talking to Martouf by the sound of things.

It had been a very trying day for her. Jordan's escapade this morning, to his fight with Janice's husband Scott and right up to what her father had done. She didn't think it was ever going to end. Never mind what was going on with her. It would have been months before she'd have found out. She wondered if Richard would have told her if he hadn't been trying to stop her from going with them to get Charlotte back. She doubted it.

Then there was Charlotte. The wording her father had used before he left the house. There was just something about it that kept niggling at her. How would he have known that Charlotte would be asleep? Had he somehow been to see her first and used the same sleeping draught he had used on Jordan? It was possible especially since Jordan had been able to flash straight to her. What was there to stop her father from doing the same? Granted he couldn't flash himself but he knew enough people that could. Even those unsavoury characters would do it for the right price.

What may have been her father's reasoning for it? She knew exactly what sleeping draught he had blown in Jordan's face. One of the most powerful ones that there were. It contained power enhancers but they only worked on witches. If Charlotte was a descendant of witches the sleeping draught would bring any powers she had to the forefront. Her not being in the Human Realm would speed that along. What was her father up too?

"Want a coffee?" Richard asked rubbing his hand up and down her arm.

"Please," Isabella replied placing a kiss on the hand that had stopped on her shoulder.

"Richard?" she called as he got to the kettle, something caught her attention.

"Yeah?" he answered placing their mugs on the side and filling them.

"Who had triplets in the Elvin Realm?"

"Nobody?" he said resting his back against the side and frowning.

"Really?" she said raising her eyebrows at his frown.

"Yes really. As far as I know there has never been a set of triplets born. Why?"

"No reason," she mindlessly replied. She picked up a book that she would have sworn had not been there earlier. The book looked new and was not the same design as the others. This one wasn't leather bound and it had gold lettering.

"What's that?" Richard asked as he placed her mug down beside her.

"A new book."

"The Mystical Triplets of the Elvin Realm. Why is it different from the others?"

"You're asking me?" she said as she watched him take a seat next to her at the table. "You know more about how the Realms work. Maybe it's for the next gener…. hold that thought."

She dropped the book quickly on the table, like it had burned her and grabbed the family tree. Isabella took a quick glance at it and then looked at her husband.

"Would you go up and check on Jordan?"

"Why? I'm sure he's fine."

"Richard. We don't know exactly what my father did to him," she lied. "So please can you go up and check on our son?"

"Fine," he huffed as he got out of his seat.

"Thank you," she said and smiled sweetly at him as he left the room.

She knew he would be fine she just wanted to make sure he was still there and hadn't flashed back to Charlotte.

"Told you he was fine," he said with a frown. It was the frown that gave Isabella pause.

"If he's fine then why are you frowning?"

"Did he have scratches on his back earlier?"

"Scratches?" she asked cocking her eyebrow.

"Yeah. Like the ones I get when you get carried away."

He couldn't help the half smile that crossed his lips. After thirty-five years of marriage he could still make her blush. Isabella was slightly stunned but after three attempts to say something she finally found her voice.

"Well. My Father did tell him to do whatever it was they were compelled to do." She really didn't know what else to say, never mind what to think.

"Yeah well. Charlotte should cut her bloody nails," Richard stated as he left the room. Isabella pressed her lips together tightly to stop the snigger from escaping at her husband's words.

Chapter Thirty-Four

Charlotte returned to consciousness with a big smile on her face. She laid there with her eyes closed basking in the afterglow of what she and Jordan had just done. Even if it had been just a dream. To her it had been a dream come true and it had felt so real.

She could still feel where their bodies had met, his lips, his hands. She bit her lip and blushed as she remembered where something else had been too. Tingles of delight swept through her body. It was only then did she notice how sore she felt down there and it gave her cause for concern. Panic started to consume her even though she was sure it had only been a dream. There was no way she should be able feel the after effects in the waking world. If that was indeed what she was feeling.

Had Vincent taken her while she slept?

As that thought registered in her mind her eyes snapped open and she sat up in the bed. The rising panic consumed her and she could feel her heart beating faster in her chest as she looked at her surroundings. This wasn't the room she'd been in before. With the colours of red and gold surrounding her the room screamed seduction even down to the white rug in front of the fireplace.

Where the hell was she now and how did she get here? Getting up onto her knees she was relieved to find she was still fully clothed in her jeans and Jordan's jumper. That had to be a good sign.

Charlotte breathed out slowly as she realised that this was the very room that had been in her dream. How? She'd never seen this room before in her life until now so unless Jordan had…? Anger and jealousy raged through her before she could even finish the thought.

"Get a grip," she muttered as she slid off the crumpled red and black satin sheets. The plush red carpet felt totally divine under her feet, she just had to wriggle her toes.

"Okay think," she said as she started pacing and tapping her finger on her lips. "There has to be a perfectly good explanation for everything. Vincent must have brought me in here after he knocked me out—bastard hit me again. Hang on, I'd been hysterical and you have to slap people when they are like that."

She stopped pacing and clutched her stomach tightly remembering why she was so hysterical earlier that day. The events flashed through her mind.

"Jordan," she breathed. Charlotte's legs gave out under her, a sharp pain shot through her as her knees slammed to the floor. She watched Jordan get hit with a bolt of light which was shot from Vincent's hands. He fell to the floor just before a bloke in black turned up and disappeared taking Jordan along with him. It had happened so fast she started to doubt that it had happened at all.

"Hang on," she said and frowned. She stood from her position on the floor still thinking about the events of the day. "I was still in the other room when grand-dad Tristan turned up. I'm almost sure he wasn't a ghost? You can't hug a ghost, can you?"

Charlotte started pacing again and racking her brain over everything that just happened. Waking up in the room from her dream had really knocked her for six.

"He said he was going to send Jordan to me and I was to do what was in my heart to do," she said blushing at the memory. "So, I did. At least I have the memory of him even if he is…. What the hell was in that weird drink Grand-dad Tristan gave me?" Her head pounded as she tried to recall the memory of his sudden visit.

Charlotte heard the door handle turn so she spun around to find a very pissed off Vincent.

"What the hell are you doing in here?"

"I don't know?"

"What do you mean you don't know?" he said stepping further into the room. "I've been looking all over the bloody castle for you."

"Worried your hostage escaped after you killed Jordan?" she snapped and cut a glance his way.

"I didn't kill Jordan," he said and couldn't hide the regret from his voice.

"You didn't?"

"No," Vincent exclaimed raising his eyebrows.

Before Charlotte could think of what she was doing her feet were moving. She wrapped her arms around Vincent's waist and was crying tears of joy. Vincent stood there like stone because he hadn't expected that reaction.

"Didn't get the chance too."

"What?" Charlotte said and realised what she was doing. She moved away from Vincent so fast she stumbled and Vincent automatically reached out to stop her fall.

"Mattias flashed with him before I could. Worst luck."

"You really are a bastard," she spat with disgust lacing every word.

"Why?" Vincent said folding his arms over his chest. "For stating the truth? If my nephew is stupid enough to put himself in such a vulnerable position, then he deserves everything he gets. It also proves something else."

"And what is that?"

"There's no way he can rescue you by flashing," Vincent said smirking like a Cheshire cat.

"What about that other bloke?" Charlotte asked absently.

"What bloke?"

"The one that came and got him? Mattias or whatever you called him?" Vincent's smirk suddenly turned into a scowl.

"Shit. Didn't think of that." Vincent muttered as he stormed out of the room.

Charlotte sat on the red velvet settee with her arm on the arm rest she placed her chin in her hand and watched Vincent leave the room with a smug look of her own on her face.

Chapter Thirty-Five

Richard dropped his mug smashing it on the floor and his coffee went everywhere.

"What the hell are you two doing here?" he growled. Mattias and Martouf had just appeared in front of him.

They just looked at each other and shrugged. Neither one cared in the slightest that they had almost scared the life out of their King.

"We had news that might be concerning," Martouf replied.

"You couldn't have used the mirrors?" Richard snapped as he pushed past them to retrieve the dustpan and brush.

"We felt it should be mentioned in person."

Richard looked both of his generals over. Mattias was dressed in the clothes that he usually wore. Martouf on the other hand was in jeans and -was that a silk shirt? He smirked and pointed at Martouf.

"You just wanted to go to the pub."

"Can't blame a guy for trying," Martouf shrugged.

"Here," Richard said as he handed the dustpan and brush to Mattias.

"What the hell am I meant to do with these?"

"Clean up the mess you caused." Richard held back the snicker as Mattias crouched down mumbling. He turned his attention back to Martouf. "So, do you actually have news or was that just an excuse?"

"No, we actually have—"

"Mattias, how lovely to see you again," Jessica practically squealed. Richard really didn't like how her face had brightened up.

Mattias stood up so fast the contents of the dustpan fell back to the floor. "Jessica," he said as he bowed before bending back down to clean up the mess once again.

Richard hadn't failed to notice the way Mattias had greeted his daughter by name and not title which wasn't like him at all. He looked at Mattias in his crouched position and back to his daughter and his gut clenched. Could her face be any brighter?

"Who are you?" Jessica asked the tall man she hadn't met yet.

Martouf turned to face the charming woman standing a foot away from him. He bowed slightly before addressing her, "I am Martouf, Princess." He lifted her hand gently and brought it too his lips. "Your humble servant." When his lips connected with her hand a growl was heard. Their heads all spun in that direction. Mattias slowly stood from completing his task and cleared his throat.

"You have got to be fucking kidding me," said Richard with frustration as he ran his hand through his hair.

"Martouf?" Isabella said surprised to see him.

"Isabella," Martouf exclaimed as he pulled her into an embrace. "When are, you going to leave the loser. And run away with me?" he said nodding his head towards Richard.

"I'm sure your beloved would love that," she said and playfully slapped his arm.

"Ah yes. My darling Kynthia." He placed his hand on his heart and smiled. "She wouldn't know. We could just blame Richard," he said with a wink.

"You're terrible," she said with a shake of her head. "What are you both doing here?"

"We had some news for Richard."

"Dressed like that?" she said looking over his attire.

"I was also hoping to go to the pub."

"Jessica go and wake up your brother." Isabella ordered before gesturing towards the dining room table. "Richard, be a darling and make coffees," she said smiling sweetly at her husband before taking a seat of her own.

"We should come here more often," Martouf said elbowing Mattias. "The King waiting on us. You don't see that every day."

"Shut it," Richard snapped playfully as he headed towards the kettle.

Ten minutes later everyone was seated around the table with coffees in hand.

"So, what's this news?" Richard asked Martouf from across the table. He was getting slightly aggravated by Jordan's constant shoulder rolling. It was all he had done since sitting at the table.

"It has been brought to our attention that Vincent has been spending a lot of time at the winter palace."

"Shouldn't Lantash be here?" Jordan asked arching his back and scrunching up his face in pain.

"Jordan. Will you stop fucking fidgeting?" Richard snapped.

"My back is stinging," sneered Jordan.

"Well tell Charlotte to cut her bloody nails then," Richard snapped. He enjoyed the surprised look on his son's face. Not to mention the stunned look on everyone else's faces.

"You were saying Martouf." Isabella interjected.

"Right," he replied clearing his throat. "Well, it has been brought to our attention that Vincent has been spending a lot of time at the winter palace."

"Lampros?" Richard enquired raising his eyebrow.

"No. All Lampros knows is that Vincent will disappear for weeks at a time and nobody knows where he has gone. It has only been in the last six months that he's been back at the autumn castle."

"Where the hell has he been then?"

"Your guess is as good as mine," Martouf shrugged. "We knew he was back in the realm but nobody had seen him." He glanced at Jordan briefly before continuing. "That was until he turned up with Charlotte."

"Then my brother was after Jessica. Why would my brother be associating with the Winter Elves? He knows as well as I that they will not listen to him, any more they do me."

"Aren't you the King?" Jessica stated bluntly.

"Yes, but these particular elves are believers of the old ways."

"Meaning what?" Jessica asked.

"Meaning that they are racist bastards," Isabella chimed in.

"As your Mother so bluntly put it they believe that the species should not mix and mingle. Elves should be with Elves and no other race. The fact that Vincent and I haven't done so is a big no no in their eyes."

"What did you guys do?" Jessica asked.

"Vincent bound himself to a Fae Princess. The fact she was his soul mate didn't matter to them, she was not an Elf. I on the other hand made things worse." Richard's eyes glazed over when he remembered times long ago and the sorrow that followed.

"How?" Jessica asked as she scooted her chair closer to her fathers.

"Ark at her," Richard said nodding in his daughter's direction. "Now she wants to know some family history. It must sound like juicy gossip."

"Daddy," Jessica said in the little girl voice most girls use to get around their Daddy's.

"Fine. Long before I even became King I was romantically involved with a witch for a very long time. That was bad enough but binding myself to a human, who in their eyes is the lowest of the low was 'the straw that broke the camel's back,' so to speak."

"But mum's part Fae."

"Yes, she is. But being born in the Human Realm makes her human as it does with Jordan, yourself and your sisters."

Richard's heart almost stopped at the realisation of what he just said. The next King of the Elves was going to be human, this would be very bad in their eyes. It also meant that he had to get back to the Elvin Realm.

"Right," Richard said clapping his hands together. "We are not going to accomplish anything here. Those who need to, get your shit together. Martouf. You and Mattias head back to Elvin Realm and get a room organised for Jessica."

"Wait! What about my boys?" Jessica asked in a panic. Mattias growled which brought everyone's attention to him once again.

"I'll go and ring Janice to come and watch them. Until your father can bring them to you." Isabella replied leaving the room.

Richard glared at Mattias as all the men in the room stood.

"Martouf?"

"Yes. Your Majesty."

"Make sure my daughter's room is next to mine," Richard ordered not taking his eyes off Mattias.

"Yes. Your Majesty." Martouf snickered as he was flashed from the room by a grumbling Mattias.

"Why can't Mattias just go and get Charlotte?" Jessica asked as she stood up.

"What?" Richard asked raising his eyebrows at her question.

"Why do we need to fight to get her back? Mattias can just flash to go and get her."

Richard just stood there realising he hadn't even considered that. With Charlotte being Jordan's soul mate he automatically assumed that he would be the one to retrieve her. However, having a plan B never hurt anyone.

"It's not a bad idea?" interrupted Jordan as Isabella walked in with her coat.

"What's not a bad idea?" Isabella asked.

"Mattias going to get charlotte," Jessica chimed in.

"The hell it is," Isabella snapped throwing her coat across the chair and table.

"It makes sense. He can flash in there and back out with her before anyone even knows what hit them," stated Jordan from his spot in the kitchen.

"Does it?"

"Yes. A good leader will use the resources he has available to him." Jordan raised his chin and tried not to falter under his mother's murderous glare. Hell, even his dad was standing still like a statue so he didn't gain her attention.

"So, your brilliant plan is to get somebody else to rescue Charlotte?" Isabella said with a deadly tone.

"It was Jessica's plan," Jordan stated pointing at his sister.

"It was just an idea," Jessica retorted scrunching up her nose.

Isabella could feel the grin on her lips. That little argument wasn't going to work this time. Not that it did when they were little.

Isabella started stalking toward her son. "So, your plan is to send someone else to get your woman?"

"Mattias would be quicker and if Dad—"

"I don't care what your father says or thinks. Mattias is *not* getting Charlotte."

Jordan glanced at his father who just shrugged at him and left the room with his sister in tow.

"Why? She would be back within minutes." His back hit the kitchen side. He hadn't even realised he had been backing away from his mother.

"And what would that say about you?" Isabella's voice was deathly calm. Which as far as Jordan was concerned was worse than if she'd been yelling. It was the calm before the storm.

"It would say I was a resourceful leader." Jordan's voice wavered under his mother's thunderous glare. Yep, the calm before the storm. He was seriously in the shit this time.

"It would say that the future King of the Elves is nothing but a coward. I didn't raise a coward."

"No, it wouldn't. It would say that I am a resourceful leader." Jordan said desperately trying to stand his ground.

"Maybe if you flashed to go and get her."

"Well I tried that and almost got myself killed."

"Because the resourceful leader didn't listen to his elders like he should have." Isabella pointed her finger in his face. "Now you are going to listen to me and do as you are bloody told."

"Yes Mother," sulked Jordan. He was pinned up against the side for so long his back had started to hurt. Thirty years old and he was still scared of his mother. How the hell did that happen?

"You my son are the future King of the Elves and have a lot to prove, given your ancestry. Especially to the older elves. If your Uncle has in fact gotten the Winter Elves involved, you will have to do more than just prove yourself." Isabella moved back from her son. "Now once we get back to the Elvin Realm if you want to flash to get Charlotte back by all means do so, that's the easy way out. But I bet you a pound to a penny that Vincent has taken measures to prevent just that. Hell, send Mattias if you have too just to prove me right—"

"Mother—"

"I'm not finished," she said giving her son the look that said don't interrupt me again. "Now, once we get back to the Elvin Realm you are going to listen to your father. When it finally comes to getting Charlotte that is your job. She is your soul mate. If you have to fight an army of Elves and god knows what else to get to her then you are bloody well going to do it. My son is not a coward and nor are you going to act like one. Did you not notice how medieval the Elvin Realm was? You have to think like those Kings from centuries ago who took on armies to get what they wanted."

"Mum, that's hardly the same thing."

"Really? So, there hasn't been a single war fought in our entire history that didn't involve some bloke getting his woman back at all costs?" Isabella was set to throw 'Helen of Troy' at her son. Myth or not, it still proved her point.

"I'm sure there has been. I will prove that I will be a good King."

"Good, just don't get yourself killed by any rash actions in the process," Isabella said as she went to retrieve her coat from the table. "Now I'm going to pick up Janice and the girls. I want you ready to go by the time I get back."

"Yes Mum." What else could he say? He watched his mother leave the room before joining his father and sister in the lounge room.

Chapter Thirty-Six

A few hours later Richard stood outside Rose Manor with Isabella, Jordan and Jessica. They were awaiting Mattias' arrival. They were flashing to the Elvin Realm and had told Janice they were getting picked up. She wasn't ready to hear the truth. It was definitely a lot easier than having to deal with his daughter's frantic ranting. Especially if they had suddenly disappeared from the house using the mirrors and would be less suspicious with no car being taken.

"When did I become your bloody taxi service?" Mattias grumbled once he flashed in front of them making them all jump.

"Did you want to explain to my -would be hysterical- daughter how we just vanished without a trace?"

"Not particularly." Mattias stated. He'd had enough of hysterical females. His ears were still ringing from Charlotte's hysterics. Holding his arms out in front of him he said, "Right, grab on."

Everyone in the group grabbed onto his arms. Tingles ran up his arm from where Jessica had hold of him but he brushed it aside and flashed.

Within seconds they had been transported to the war room of the main Elfin Castle. Richard grabbed for Mattias as he started to stumble. The amount of flashing he had done must have been getting the better of him. Richard noticed Martouf and Lantash were standing by the wall. He stood there stunned as Lantash walked straight to Jessica ignoring everyone else in the room.

"Princess Jessica." Lantash bowed at her feet and grabbed her hand, resting his forehead on it. "It is an honour." Mattias growled and Lantash snarled at him.

Richard looked between his two generals. What the hell had gotten into them? His daughter couldn't possibly have two potential soul mates. It wasn't unheard of, just very rare. Now he wished he had brought the family tree with him instead of leaving it on the dining room table. That thought gave him pause and he realised he had forgotten about the books as well. What if Janice had a look through everything on the table? He shrugged to himself and thought 'Fuck it, she'll find out soon enough anyway.' It would be just another thing he had to deal with later. Right now, he had more pressing matters.

"Martouf."

"Yes your Majesty." Martouf bowed at Richard and tried not to snigger at his colleague's actions.

"Jessica's quarters are ready. I presume?"

"Yes, your Majesty."

"Right, would you kindly escort *my daughter* to them and retrieve her in an hour. Her training will start then." Richard put emphasis on his words and looked between Mattias and Lantash who had only now removed themselves from his daughter.

"This way Princess." Martouf bowed slightly and headed towards the door. A stunned Jessica following in his wake.

"Isabella my love. How about you go and see your parents." Richard placed a kiss on her forehead. "Or have a lie down before dinner. It's going to be a long afternoon." Isabella nodded at her husband and left the room.

Richard turned his attention to the remaining three in the room.

"You three go change your gear, then I want you in the training room. You have ten minutes," he ordered as he left the room.

Chapter Thirty-Seven

Jordan stood along the wall of the training hall in the main Elfin Castle next to his father. They were awaiting the first lesson in Jessica's training. Both were in battle gear. However, Jordan had chosen an olive singlet and camouflage combat paints. His long hair was flowing over his shoulders except for the top half which was pulled back into a pony tail. His sister had made some comment about looking like Tommy from the Power Rangers but he hadn't quite caught exactly what she had said.

He looked at his father standing there in all his elfin glory. He stood with his legs apart and arms folded across his chest. He stared intently at Jessica as she picked up a sword to train with Martouf. Jordan was glad when his sister had finally stopped staring at their father with her gob open.

His attention was drawn back to his sister and he couldn't help the laugh that erupted from his chest as he watched Jessica try to lift the broadsword and dropping it instantly.

"What you laughing at?" Jessica asked looking at her brother.

"You," Jordan replied.

"And what's so funny?" she asked as she put her hands on her hips to glare at him. Her long black T-shirt just rising slightly over her black leggings.

"Those swords are for warriors. Try one of those light weight cutlasses," Jordan replied smirking.

"Up yours!" Jessica replied with a un-lady like two finger gesture before turning to the smaller swords and picking one up.

He watched Jessica's sword play with Martouf and he couldn't believe how bad she was faring. Martouf was constantly disarming her.

His dad kept shaking his head and hiding his expression behind his hands and it was doing his head in. He knew Jessica was better than what they were seeing.

Jordan looked over at his Dad. "What is it?" he asked.

"We can't take Jessica with us to a battle ground as much as she wants to help get Charlotte back. It would be like taking a lamb to slaughter," Richard answered not taking his eyes off his daughter.

"This is bullshit." Jordan suddenly snapped.

"What is?" Richard asked looking at Jordan.

"I know Jessica is better than this."

"I can't see how," Richard replied raising an eyebrow.

"Watch this," Jordan replied before turning his attention to his sister. "Oi, Obi-Wan!"

Jessica stopped dead mid-strike and looked at her brother. "What?"

"Pretend he's Vader for Christ sake," he said gesturing to Martouf.

"But your always Vader," she replied.

"Oh, for god sake just pick a Star Wars bad guy will you," he said exasperated.

Jessica smiled and her whole body shifted. She brought her sword down and not only caught Martouf totally off guard, she even managed to get the upper hand in the sword fight. With a few smooth moves and a bit of twirling she had disarmed him and knocked him on his arse with a high kick to the chest.

"What just happened?" Richard asked not quite knowing how his daughter went from hopeless at sword fighting to getting the upper hand over his best swordsman.

Jordan smiled with pride. He knew his sister could fight. "Why do you think Mum had to keep replacing the broom handles? Jessica and I would snap them when we pretended they were light sabres."

"I did wonder why some of the moves she pulled looked familiar and I suppose she knows martial arts from watching Power Rangers."

"Well, Tommy any way," Jordan said not stopping the laugher rumbling in his chest. He loved how stunned everyone looked.

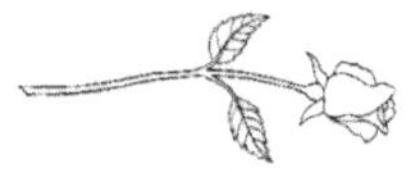

Jessica looked down at a very startled looking Martouf. She couldn't help feeling proud of herself after knocking him on his arse.

"You okay?" she asked as she extended a hand to help him up.

"Yeah," he replied grabbing her hand. Once on his feet he brushed himself off then turned to Jessica. "You did well my young padawan."

"You know Star Wars?" Jessica asked in shock.

"Yeah and I hate to think what villain you were picturing me as. You know what? Go with that, whatever works to get the job done. The enemy is going to think that you're a helpless damsel, an easy target. So, you have you're element of surprise."

"Sweet," Jessica beamed.

"Next!" Martouf turned away from Jessica and made his way over to join Richard and Jordan. He felt embarrassed that she had managed to best him, but pride as well. He had confidence that if she could do that to him she could do that to anyone. Just the sheer surprise of it would be her attack move.

"Hey Dad!" Jessica shouted while Lantash took his place on the mat before her.

"What sweetheart?"

"Can I get one of those Xena suits?"

"What Xena suit?" Richard asked frowning at her.

"You know. In the show. The same out-fit she has."

"That is hardly suitable battle gear."

"So, what would I be wearing then?"

Richard stood there not having a clue how to answer her question. Even though there were now female warriors in the kingdom they didn't actually have any armour that was strictly for the girls.

"What would you have in mind?"

"Well, something like the Xena out-fit. You know, with one of those breast knife things and one that goes into your hair," Jessica said pulling her hair into a half-up, half-down style. "If the enemy gets too close or your laying a trap for them you can pull the knife from your hair."

"After your training with Lantash go and discuss it with Trixie. Then head to your training with Mattias." Richard didn't like the sound of the last part. He hoped she wouldn't get that close to an enemy.

"Will do," she said turning to face Lantash. "I'm learning to fight with those triton things?"

"There called Sai," Lantash said holding the weapons out to her. "Technically you won't be learning to fight with them at all."

"So, what will I be learning then?" she said in confusion.

"Princess. You will be learning to block and disarm."

"Is this going to be a lengthy lesson?"

"No. Just the basics and enough to get you out of trouble. After all, being from the Fae Realm if you do end up stuck at all you can just flash to get away."

"Which is what you will be doing," Richard chimed in.

Jessica just rolled her eyes. "So basically, you are going to come at me with another weapon and I use those to stop you," she said while grabbing the weapons being handed to her.

Jessica checked them out and barely had time to process what was happening when out of the corner of her eye she caught site of Lantash heading towards her with a raised sword. She automatically turned her body and put her arms above her head crossed. She barely stopped the sword hitting her as she fell on her back with Lantash landing on top of her.

"What the hell was that?" she practically screeched as a loud roar spread through the room.

"Just checking your reflexes," Lantash said smiling at her. He was clearly enjoying the position he was currently in.

"How'd I do?"

"Could have been better," he answered and raised his body slightly, freeing up her legs.

Jessica gave him her most sweet and innocent smile.

"How's this for a reflex?" she said bringing her leg up so her thigh roughly met his groin.

"Good," he choked out. It was clear he was in pain as he rolled off her.

Jessica sat up and looked around the room to see where the roar had come from. All she saw was her dad and brother with Mattias. They were about two feet away from her. When had they gotten there? She was about to ask when Mattias stormed out of the training room.

"Where is Mattias going?" she asked her father.

"To set up the cross-bow targets." He looked at Lantash. "You, in my office NOW."

"Yes your Majesty." Lantash got up and bowed before leaving the room.

"Is that it for my lessons?" she asked dusting off her leggings.

"No, since you are only being shown the basics your brother can teach you."

"Oh, okay then," she said bending down to pick up her weapons.

"Jordan, teach her the basics. I don't care how you do it, just make sure she gets it." Jordan nodded at his father. "Martouf get Mattias and meet me in my office."

"On it." Martouf hurried out of the room as he had never seen his old friend look so pissed off before.

"An hour of solid training then go get cleaned up and see Trixie about the armour for the women. I will meet you both in the grand hall for dinner," he said addressing his children and they both nodded.

"How much more shit is going to happen?" he muttered as he left the training room.

Chapter Thirty-Eight

Richard stood at the window of his office which was more like an arched hole in the wall. He stood with his back to the room while he waited for Martouf and Mattias to arrive. He had seen his sister in passing and grabbed her for the unplanned meeting. It was just unfortunate she was going to be witnessing a bollocking as well.

"We're here." Martouf announced as he entered the room with Mattias following closely behind him. Trixie and Lantash joined them at the other side of his desk.

Richard couldn't help but feel like he was the nasty teacher about to give the naughty students the cane. They were all standing in a neat row, two of them had their heads down and it was the first thing he thought of.

"Trixie, Martouf if you two wouldn't mind taking a seat over there," he said as he gestured to the leather settee that sat to the left of his desk. "I have something unpleasant to deal with before we get started."

He watched them take their seats and turned to cast a stern look at the two who were left standing in front of him. He hated to reprimand anyone but the way these two had been towards each other since Jessica's arrival was going to cause a fight. He couldn't have that and it only seemed to happen when they were around his daughter. If one of them dared to growl or snarl at him where his daughter was concerned, then there would be hell to pay.

"What the fucking hell has gotten into you two?" Richard leaned forward and placed his fisted hands on the desk waiting for his answer. "Well, don't all speak at once?"

"Don't know," they both said at once.

"You don't know, well let me enlighten you, shall I? Ever since meeting my daughter you have both been acting like…. I don't know …Horny teenagers or possessive alpha males. You are both over two-hundred-years-old not fucking fifteen."

Richard slowly stalked around his desk and stood in front of Lantash.

"What the fuck was that in the training room?"

"What was what?" Lantash said not making eye contact with the king.

"That stunt you pulled."

"I was testing her reflexes, to see—"

"Did you do the same with Jordan?"

"God no," Lantash answered before thinking. He made eye contact with his King and winced. At that moment, he wished it was his king and not an angry father.

Richard raised his eyebrows at that remark. "Lantash."

"Yes your Majesty."

"I am going to say this only once. Unless my daughter turns out to be your soul mate." Mattias growled again which earned him another glare from Richard. "If you EVER pull a stunt like that again with my daughter it won't be a friend or king you deal with but an angry father and I will have your head. Do I make myself clear?"

"Yes your Majesty," Lantash said stopping suddenly when his back hit the wall. When had he started backing away from Richard? Why was Richard only inches from his face?

"Now go and wait with the others." Not giving Lantash a chance to reply he turned his attention to an awaiting Mattias. "And you," he said letting the words draw out slowly.

Mattias turned slowly and faced Richard not saying a word. He looked at him dead in the eyes.

"How long is it going to be before you rip somebody's throat out?"

"What?" Mattias had no idea what Richard was going on about.

"You've been growling like some wild fucking animal every time a male goes near my daughter."

"No I haven't."

Richard raised his eyebrows in shock at Mattias. "Yes, you have. Lantash, Martou—"

"He didn't growl at you," Martouf chimed in and Richard spun on his heel to face him.

"I hadn't mentioned that yet but might have had you not butted in," he said. Richard turned to face Mattias again. "And I will have his head if he does. Is that clear?"

"Yes."

"Good. If you have the slightest inkling that you may be my daughters' soul mate, then I want to know about it. Until then both you and Lantash will stay away from her."

"Yes your Majesty," Mattias said through clenched teeth. He really didn't like being given those orders which only added to his ever-growing confusion.

Richard just raised his eyebrow at him. "And another thing, where the hell did that burst of speed come from in the training room?" Richard had never seen Mattias move so fast. He wouldn't have beaten him to Lantash had he not been paying close attention to his friend's movements. He had been making his way slowly toward him when Lantash had joined Jessica on the training mat.

"I honestly don't know and to be honest it's gotten me a little nervous." Mattias didn't see any point in not being honest with his long-time friend.

"Flash to Charlotte," Richard suddenly ordered.

"And do what?"

"Just flash to where she is and then come back on your own."

"Why?" everyone said at once.

"I want to check something."

Mattias shrugged and flashed from the room. Within seconds he was back in the office and being flung across the room. He hit the wall and landed in a heap on the floor. "What the fuck?"

"That's what I thought," Richard said rubbing his cheek and helping Mattias up from the floor.

"Care to share?" Mattias said and winced from the pain that shot through his body. "Thanks."

"Isabella suggested that Vincent might have done something to prevent flashing."

"And I was your test subject? Thanks."

"Sorry," Richard said shrugging. "Now, you mentioned that Vincent has been spending a lot of time at the winter elves palace?"

"Yes. We don't know why, but thought it might be of some importance." Martouf answered.

"Do we know if he is there now?"

"Not a clue," Martouf answered shrugging.

"Well I think it's time I pay my little brother a visit."

"What about Charlotte?" Trixie asked.

"If Vincent gives her up, great. However, I have a feeling this goes deeper than just having Charlotte. Trixie, you meet up with Jessica to get those out-fits sorted." Richard looked at his other generals, "You three are with me."

Chapter Thirty-Nine

Richard reached the edge of the autumn forest. He hadn't actually seen the castle since the day he had almost demolished it getting Jordan back. The renovations had clearly gone well. To look at it, a person would never believe that half the castle wall had fallen to the ground not from this distance any way. As Richard approached the castle itself however the renovations could be clearly seen.

Reaching the castle gate Richard stopped in front of the two young Elves on duty. He knew these two as he had met them before.

"Nicodemus, Iolaus."

"Your Majesty," both Elves replied bowing towards Richard.

"Is Prince Vincent in residence?"

"No, your Majesty," Iolaus answered. "General Lampros is here though."

"Could you go and get him for me please."

"Yes your Majesty." Iolaus bowed and entered the castle. He returned a short while later with General Lampros.

"Your Majesty," Lampros said as he bowed.

"Lampros. Where is my brother?"

"He's gone to the winter palace."

"And Charlotte?" Richard enquired with a raised brow.

"He took her with him. He left in a black carriage this morning."

"Carriage?"

"Yep. A horse drawn one would you believe?" Lampros sounded as surprised as Richard felt.

"No, I wouldn't. Considering our realm shouldn't have either." Richard looked over at the forest leading to the winter palace. "Why did Vincent take Charlotte with him? Why not just leave her here?"

"I asked him the same thing."

"And?" Richard asked prompting Lampros to continue.

"I couldn't be trusted with Charlotte." Richard raised his eyebrows. "Not like that. Vincent was more concerned with me returning the girl. I think he has decided to keep her."

"Well he can't have her," Richard exclaimed.

"What are we going to do now?" Martouf enquired from Richard's side.

"We are taking a trip to the winter palace it would seem," Richard glanced at each of his general's. "It's going to be a long walk so we should make a move."

"We're not grabbing supplies or anything?" Lantash asked.

"No. We will use our elf speed and get there in half the time."

"But the winter palace. Have you forgotten its bloody freezing in that part of the realm?"

Richard turned to face Lantash completely.

"No I haven't. However, after the long walk we have ahead of us it won't be as cold. So, stop you're bitching and let's go." Without another word, Richard turned and headed towards the forest at the edge of the Autumn Castle grounds. It didn't take long before a muttering Lantash stormed past him across the green grass while Martouf and Mattias came up beside him and matched him step for step. Richard glanced briefly at Mattias and suddenly stopping dead in his tracks.

"Lantash, hold up," Richard yelled. He watched his friend stomp his way back over to him.

"What did you call me back for?" Lantash said scowling at Richard.

"I didn't," Richard scolded. "I just told you to hold up. There is a difference." Lantash shrugged at Richard. "Any way, you know what I forgot?"

"That Mattias can flash." Martouf and Lantash chorused. Richard just scowled at them both.

Mattias stood there with his hands in his pockets looking at his feet. His mind was clearly on other things. Knowing that all eyes were on him he looked up and answered. "No."

"Why the hell not?" stomped Lantash.

"Where the hell is that Charlotte woman?"

"She's at the castle," Richard answered.

"Then no. I'm not flashing us. Last time I was sent flying across the room. This time I could be catapulted for miles." Mattias turned and headed for the forest.

"You don't have to flash us into the castle," Richard interjected.

"Then where?" Mattias said and just kept walking.

"To the outskirts of the forest. Odds are, Vincent only has her where Charlotte is shielded from flashing." Mattias turned and cocked one eyebrow at his king. "There is also the fact that we will be with you, so if you're flung for miles, so will we be."

Mattias liked that idea.

"I guess I'm flashing us then?" he grinned, making his way back to the others. "Where exactly?"

"The edge of the forest. It would give us the element of surprise. Vincent could have scouts scattered around the forest for all we know and they could alert him to our presence." Martouf interjected.

"Don't we want Vincent to know where coming?" Lantash asked rather confused.

"No. With him spending most of his time at the winter palace knowing that the elves in the area have a deep hate for both myself and Vincent, I would rather surprise him. He might panic and with any luck do something stupid," Richard stated.

"Let's go then," Mattias said holding out his arms once again. Each elf grabbed onto his arm and within seconds they were gone.

Chapter Forty

Charlotte clutched her stomach as Vincent escorted her from the carriage. The ride had been so bumpy she was surprised she hadn't been sick yet. They had been traveling for a few hours along what felt like a stone road that obviously hadn't been laid very well. Curiosity got the better of her and she glanced a look back to where they had come from. Yep the road was indeed made of stone and there were elves shovelling the snow to the edges.

It was no wonder she had an upset stomach as she rarely got travel sickness. Except for that one time in America when she was visiting her brother and his wife. That time had also been due to a horse drawn carriage.

"Note to self, no horse drawn carriage for my wedding," she muttered looking at the horse. It was a beautiful black horse with a regal mane and a long tail that almost touched the ground. Charlotte thought he was magnificent.

She had also been surprised that Vincent was a pleasant travel companion. He hadn't even tried anything during the journey. Since his plan was to seduce her she thought the dark carriage would have been the ideal place. It's not like she could have gotten very far if she had tried to escape.

"This way my dear," Vincent said bringing her out of her thoughts.

Charlotte glanced up at the castle wall. It was cold stone just like any other.

"Why is this place called the winter palace? It's just a stone castle like any other," she asked.

"I don't know," Vincent shrugged and turned to face her. "I guess it sounded better. You were expecting something else?"

"Yes, I was actually," Charlotte said glancing up at the castle again. "Like what?"

"Well…. Just the title of the place conjures up a beautiful image of a gorgeous palace. Like the Palace of Versailles in France, not dull and dingy stone," she said motioning to the castle with her hand. "It is rather disappointing."

Vincent rolled his eyes.

"You humans are all the same."

"Why couldn't you just leave me at the other castle," she moaned and shuddered from the chill that hit her.

"I didn't want Lampros doing the honourable thing and taking you back to Richard," Vincent huffed.

"But isn't Lampros you're guy?"

"Yes, Lampros is my general. However, he has sworn to serve the King."

"And clearly that's not you," she smirked.

"Not yet," Vincent smirked. "If my plan works that will be one situation rectified thanks to you."

"What is that supposed to mean?" she said and a feeling of dread filled her stomach.

"That means having you is going to be the icing on the cake."

"You still plan to seduce me then?"

"I have many plans for you my dear."

Charlotte had trouble swallowing the lump that had suddenly formed in her throat. That didn't sound good at all. Glancing over the snow-covered ground towards the direction they had come she wondered if she could make a run for it.

"Don't even think about it. I would catch you before you had even gotten five steps," Vincent warned. He had seen the look on her face and noticed her step back. "Now come along it's frightfully cold out here and I can't have you catching your death." He motioned for her to go ahead of him. Vincent narrowed his eyes at her back as she passed him. There was something different about her but he couldn't place what it was. He quickly shrugged it off and followed close behind her.

Charlotte didn't look around at anything on her way to the room because it was all grey stone walls. It was very boring and having Vincent constantly behind her giving her directions just pissed her off. At least twice she had spun around to give him the finger which just made him tut at her and shake his head.

"This one," Vincent said motioning to a plain wooden door with a ring for a door handle.

Charlotte looked at the ring on the door. It was one of those old-fashioned door latches. When she turned it the door slowly swung open, creaking at the hinges. She didn't think this room had been used in a while and it even looked like it at first glance.

"Is this it?" she said crunching up her nose. The room was all stone and smelled musty. The blankets on the bed looked clean even if the old looking bed didn't. And was that a chamber pot in the corner next to the changing screen?

"It will do for now. You have your basic amenities. I don't see what the problem is? Or would you rather share a bed with me?" Vincent said smirking.

"This will be fine." Charlotte exclaimed. She really didn't want to be in the same room as Vincent especially with the way he was currently eyeing her off. "Oh look, a window."

She headed over to the window and glanced outside. She could see nothing but snow which led right up to the forest edge. Charlotte gasped at what she saw and squinted to get a better look. Did she really just see four figures appear out of nowhere? In the current situation she was in, she guessed anything was possible.

Charlotte glanced at Vincent over her shoulder to see what he was doing. He seemed to be busy lighting candles and a fire in the small fireplace. She turned her attention back to the window, which was more like a fancy hole in the wall. She was sure she knew one of the figures heading towards the castle.

"Is that Richard?" she blurted without thinking and then slapped her hand over her mouth.

"What?"

"Nothing," Charlotte murmured behind her hand.

Vincent stormed over to the window and his jaw hardened when he saw the four figures.

"Damn it!" Vincent exclaimed as he rushed over to the door. He pointed at Charlotte just before he left the room, "You stay here and keep away from that window."

Charlotte jumped when the old door slammed behind him. She took a quick peak out the window before Vincent got there. She could tell it was Richard. Was he here to get her? Excitement filled her at the thought. All she wanted to do was yell and wave at him from the window but she thought that probably wasn't a great idea. She opted to stay at the window though, to hell with what Vincent said.

Chapter Forty-One

Richard shuddered at the sudden temperature drop. They had arrived in the forest on the edge of the snow field, which was part of the castle grounds. He'd forgotten it was always cold in this part of the realm. Winter all year-round. Glancing at the others he stepped out of the forest and made his way to the castle. The ankle-deep snow crunched under his foot with every step. The closer Richard got to the castle the thinner the snow appeared to be.

The path near the castle had been cleared. Possibly for the black carriage that stood just past the castle door. The grounds around the immediate area looked to have seen a lot of activity as well. It had less snow and looked more like brown sludge.

Richard glanced up at the windows and saw Charlotte standing by one of them. She was waving like mad at him but her sudden retreat from the window caught Richard's attention. Looking towards the castle door he spotted his brother. He was being followed by other supernatural beings, some of which he had never seen. Them being there was an ominous sign and threw any plans he had made straight out the window. Why the hell were they in his realm?

"Vincent," Richard said as he stopped approximately four feet away from his brother.

"Richard, to what do I owe this pleasure?" Vincent stood casually with his hands in the pockets of the long black coat he was wearing. A fake smile gracing his features.

"I've come for Charlotte."

"Well you can't have her, she's mine."

"She is Jordan's and you know it," Richard snarled.

"A problem easily solved once I rid the realm of the human prince," Vincent declared. He watched his brother's posture carefully. That last comment had gotten to him like Vincent knew it would.

Richard narrowed his eyes at his brother with his fists clenched tight in his pockets. He took a deep breath and exhaled it through his nose to try to regain some of his composure. He was the King of Elves and he knew his brother had said that deliberately to get a rise out of him. Well it was Richard's turn to play that game.

"Eager to replace Constance, are you?"

"Don't you dare say her name," Vincent said glaring at his brother.

"Constance would be displeased," Richard tilted his head slightly. "First you try and take my Isabella with whom, as you know, is your beloved late mates' baby sister."

"Don't. I'm warning you," Vincent said stepping closer to his brother.

"Then there was Sonya who just so happens to be the woman the human prince, as you put it, spent ten years with. How do you know that you haven't produced a human prince yourself with her?" Richard's casual stance was an act. He was keeping a close eye on his brother's movements as he was goading his brother's impulsive nature waiting for a bolt of light to be released.

"What would Constance think about you being after her nephew's soul mate? Not to mention how many women from the human realm that have warmed your bed over the years."

"Constance wouldn't think anything because she is dead and it's your fault." Anger surged through Vincent and without a thought he flung a bolt of light at his brother, only for it to miss.

"My fault?" Richard said placing his hand on his chest. "She was meant to have stayed in the human realm with Trixie to look after her baby brother. Instead she was jumping in the middle of a battle, for god knows what reason."

"Whose fault was it that we happened to have been in a battle?" Vincent snapped.

"Those who thought they could walk in and take our realm."

"You had the power to have wiped them out."

"Like I could with this lot," Richard said as he motioned with his head to those around Vincent.

"He wishes!" someone from the group yelled which was followed by a rumble of agreement by all present excluding the elves.

Richard cast his eyes over the crowd landing on the speaker who clearly hadn't noticed the elves around him had moved out of the way, including Vincent. They knew that the King was always the strongest in their realm.

"Really Vincent, associating with Vampires. I would have thought your little army here would consist of better. Looks like you're scraping the bottom of the barrel."

"So, wipe them out then. Use that big bad power you have and kill them all."

"And you as well?" Richard raised his eyebrows at his brother.

"What?"

"You want so badly to take my throne. You don't even know what's involved. I can take this little rabble out with a blink of an eye. However, you would be taken out as well as everyone within a two-mile radius. I don't know about you but I would much rather have Martouf, Lantash and Mattias alive. Not forgetting that little blonde you have locked in one of those rooms."

"You want the pretty blonde, then you will have to take her by force," Vincent snarled. He hadn't known about that part of his brother's powers and wasn't about to make himself look a fool by admitting it.

"So be it." Richard turned and made his way back to the forest.

"Give up the throne and she is yours now," Vincent hollered.

"What?" Richard said turning to face his brother.

"You want Charlotte so badly, give the throne to me and she is yours."

Richard just stood there, should he? Was that even possible?

"Don't you even think it?" Martouf snapped. "You know your brother is a lying bastard."

Richard glanced at Martouf then turned his gaze back to his brother.

"I don't think so. The only way you will get the throne is over mine and Jordan's dead bodies."

"That's the plan, my brother. You will see the life leave your son just before you join him."

Richard felt panic and rage build inside of him and without thinking he swung his arm in the direction of his brother. He sent a wave of power over them and knocked them on their arses, he then turned and headed for the forest once again.

"By the end of the week, the throne will be mine," Vincent yelled after his brother.

Richard faced his brother once again and gave him the two-finger salute. "Up yours," Richard exclaimed but didn't get chance to say any more. A group of the men shifted and bolted straight for them.

"Mattias. Flash us NOW," Richard ordered. Once Martouf, Richard and Lantash had grabbed onto his out stretched arms he flashed.

Chapter Forty-Two

Richard started to panic once they flashed into the court yard of the main Elvin castle. There had to be a few hundred people in the yard. Had Vincent sent some of his minions to the castle while Richard had been at the winter palace? It took him a minute or two to realise that nobody was fighting and he knew a few that had gathered. Christina, Tristan and even Ruby's family were there. However, he couldn't see Ruby or the other witch family that hadn't been with Vincent.

"What the hell is going on?" Richard asked Christina who was heading towards him as soon as she noticed they were back. Tristan and Ruby's father had also started heading his way.

"Well, my dear," she said resting her hand on his forearm. "Let's just say we have better spies in the neutral realm than you do."

"Meaning?"

"People talk when their drunk. From what my little eavesdroppers have discovered this is bigger than just getting Charlotte back."

"I rather thought it was. Even more so now that I have seen the garrison that Vincent has stashed away at the winter palace. I didn't have a clue what half of them even were. Never mind, if we even have any defences against them."

"We will work something out," she said as she gently patted his arm.

"So why is everyone else here?" Richard motioned to the other elder's present. "Tristan, I can take a guess at, but the others?"

"There has been a disturbance in the energy surrounding the Witches covens, which is why Goliath is here," Tristan said motioning to an ancient looking man. "We know the other Witch faction is at the winter palace with Vincent. They have been wanting domination over the realms since their conception. So even though some of us are here for family reasons. We also want to make sure those witches don't get a foot hold in this realm. It will have a domino effect if they do."

By this time, Isabella, Jordan and Trixie had joined the little group.

"So, what species were at the castle?" Trixie asked.

Richard looked at his sister.

"Well, there were some I didn't recognise. I did recognise the Witches, Vampires and Shift—"

"Vampires. Did they sparkle?" Trixie couldn't contain her excitement.

"Really???" Jordan growled out. "Everything is like a film to you. Next you'll be quoting Supernatural or Charmed."

"Only if the situation permits it," she snapped.

"Why the hell don't you just live in the human realm?"

"Jordan that's enough!" Richard snapped.

"Why doesn't someone just answer my bloody question?" Trixie snapped.

"No Trixie, they didn't bloody sparkle. Now can we focus? I think we have more important things to worry about now don't you? Such as the army which Vincent has amassed coming here and wiping us all out?"

"You really think it will come to that?" Isabella asked. She had never seen her husband look so worried.

"I think it's a strong possibility. I didn't know what half of the species were and only knew about five of the shifters there because they had shifted. They came after us just before we flashed back."

"Did you do something first?" Isabella said raising her eyebrow.

"I sent a shock wave over the castle and kind of knocked them all on their arses."

"So, what shifters were there that you saw?" Isabella enquired.

"From the quick glance, I got there was a wolf." Richard pointed his finger at his sister. "Don't you dare say a word to that one?" Trixie snapped her mouth shut and continued to listen. "There was also a lion and tiger. I didn't catch the other two that shifted." Richard briefly glanced at his sister, he could tell she was holding back a comment.

"Well we can assume that they have some kind of weapons training and will no doubt fight in both forms," added Isabella tapping her index finger on her lip.

"Fighting a big cat isn't easy for any species,"

"Then we fight dirty if they shift, we use our powers. You can bet your arse they will be fighting dirty," Isabella screeched. "No more mister nice king. If you have to use that Jedi thing and break their necks, then do it."

"Um, Mum," Jordan said holding his finger up.

"Don't you dare correct me on the difference between the Jedi and Sith right now." She glared at her son and Jordan clamped his mouth shut.

"Either way, we might have some preparation time. How much, god only knows. So, do we know anyone who might know something about the other supernatural beings and do we have any healers amongst us?" Richard subconsciously touched his shoulder.

"Loki?" Christina answered.

"Loki?" Richard scoffed. "He's just Rose Manor's caretaker. Even if he is a shifter of some form. What good would he do?"

Christina scowled at her son-in-law. "Do you have any idea what type of shifter he is?"

"A Unicorn?" Richard didn't care for her tone and answered her accordingly with his own.

"Your sarcasm just bit you in the arse." Christina said and couldn't wipe the smug look off her face if she tried.

"You're joking?"

"No, I'm not." Christina gathered her skirts from her long silver gown and stepped closer to Richard. "Not only is he a unicorn shifter and a bloody strong healer but he is also older than dirt. If anyone knows what those other supernatural beings are it would be him."

"We need to get him here." Richard said as he glanced over the crowd. "Mattias!"

"You can't send Mattias to go and get him," Christina added just as Mattias reached them with Jessica close behind.

"Why not?"

"Loki doesn't know Mattias. I'll go and fetch him."

Before Richard could argue with her she flashed from the court yard. He needed to get plans into motion and was clearly going to have to wing it. "Martouf!"

"Yes your Majesty."

"Get some men and start blocking off all the passages that lead to the other castles. Then post guards." Martouf bowed and started gathering the elves. "Lantash, post guards along the castle battlements and along the forest edge. Make sure you cover it in all directions."

"Yes your Majesty."

"Trixie!"

"Yes boss," she said standing next to her brother and giving him a salute.

"If those outfits for the women are ready start getting them suited and booted." Trixie nodded and grabbed Jessica's arm, shouting for the other women to join her in the castle.

Richard opened his mouth to bark more orders when Christina flashed in front of him, making him jump. He narrowed his eyes at her giggling and cast a glance over her shoulder to an angry looking Loki and his very pregnant mate.

"Oh no. What the hell is she doing here?" Richard snapped glaring at Christina.

"Loki wouldn't leave without—"

"Claire!" Isabella screeched and ran up to the newcomer pulling her into a hug. "Oh my god look at you."

"Isabella," Richard said.

"What?" she snapped at her husband.

"She's not staying," he stated flatly.

"Your husband doesn't seem to like me, does he?" Claire asked in an almost whisper.

Isabella glanced at her husband before responding. "Oh, he's still sore about the frying pan incident."

"Yeah well, it bloody hurt," Richard growled and subconsciously rubbed the back of his head. A cold shiver suddenly ran up his body. Richard turned around and was met with a very angry looking Mattias glaring daggers at a curious looking Loki. "What's going on?"

"You're not an Elf." Loki said addressing Mattias and completely ignoring Richard.

"Yeah I know. So?" Mattias said in anger. He didn't like the intense stare the newcomer was throwing his way.

"You don't know what you are do you?"

"And I suppose you do."

"I do and you are actually very rare. This would be the second time I have come across your species." Loki placed his hand on his chest and bowed. "It is an honour."

"Who were the other ones?" Richard asked just as gobsmacked as Mattias looked.

"A lovely couple on the run in the human realm from hunters." Loki straightened and continued. "They had a set of twin boys with them. That was even rarer for their species. I helped them get to the Neutral Realm via my portal at Rose Manor."

"So, what am I?" Mattias asked as curiosity got the better of him.

"A conversation for another time perhaps," he said as he turned to face Richard. "I assume I'm here for more pressing matters."

"We need your assistance but first I think we should get our guests settled in. Mattias, start getting everyone into the great hall. Get some refreshments organised and find some elves to sort out accommodations for everyone. Even if you use the old abandoned villages around the castle grounds. Also, tell them to gather their children and pregnant women. We will be moving them to safety soon and I will need your assistance." Mattias nodded at Richard and took off.

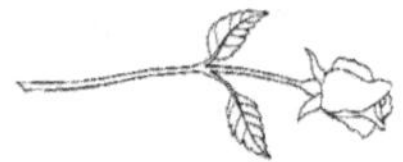

A short while later Richard sat at an iron table in the now empty court yard. It had been a lovely sunny afternoon and the last thing he wanted to do was to sit in his stuffy office or be stuck in the war room. All the children had been gathered and were now playing in the castle grounds or sitting on blankets eating ice-cream with not a care in the world. He was trying to make it seem like a normal day for the younger ones.

"Christina?"

"Yes Richard," Christina answered not taking her eyes off a group of teenage elves, fae and witches doing cartwheels. The younger ones were trying to copy them.

"How many fae do we have that are strong enough to flash to Rose Manor with passengers?"

Christina stopped watching the children and turned her gaze towards him. "Depends on the passengers and how many?"

Richard motioned to the children and pregnant women who had taken seats next to the castle in the shade.

"All fae should be able to do it. Even the weaker ones if they only do one trip, with say three children each. Isabella should be able to handle a couple of trips with about seven children. Jessica could do a few more than that. With Mattias assisting we should be able to get everyone transported within the hour."

"I can help." Jordan added a little insulted that he hadn't been mentioned.

"No," Richard answered without hesitation. "You're flashing ability will be needed here."

"For what purpose?"

"To flash Loki and myself to the winter palace so he can see the supernatural beings that I can't identify. We will be heading there while the children are being flashed to Rose Manor." Richard hoped that Jordan would be strong enough to flash within the same realm.

"Okay then," Jordan said as he took a mouthful of his lemonade.

"Actually, we should get that started Vincent could attack at any moment." Richard stood and headed towards the grass area where the children were playing. Those that were going to be flashing the passengers followed and stood two metres apart. "Kids, gather round."

Richard waited until all the children had gathered around. There must have been over one hundred children. His chest hurt at the low number of Elvin children present. He pushed it aside so he could deal with the situation in front of him. He had to make out the kids were going on an adventure so not to frighten the younger ones. He knew the older ones would have already sussed out that something serious was happening. He couldn't very well say 'Hey kids there is a war coming and you're all being evacuated'.

Crouching down he looked at the row of toddlers with ice-cream all over their faces.

"Who's been having fun?" he asked but when nobody answered he looked up and saw a sea of bobbing heads.

"That's good. Now in a few minutes' you guys are going to be going on a big adventure to the Human Realm for a few days. So, you must go say bye to Mummy and Daddy otherwise they will be very cross with me and we don't want that."

"Mummy will smack your bum," said a five-year-old elf.

Richard laughed at the little elf. "Yes, Mummy would smack my bum and I don't want that. So, go tell Mummy about the big adventure and come right back." Richard stepped back as the hoard of children ran into the castle.

It wasn't too long before the children were back. Their faces were a mixture of excitement and tears. All the younger ones had lolly-pops to keep them occupied and seemed happy enough. The older ones seemed to be keeping themselves occupied while clinging to Mattias. He knew Mattias would rather be loaded up like a donkey with twenty, five-year-olds, than with ten swooning teenagers like he had now.

"Okay are we ready?" Christina said to her bunch of children.

"Wait!" Richard yelled holding up his hand.

"What?" Christina snapped.

"Isabella goes first."

"What…Why?"

Richard stepped closer to his mother-in-law. "Janice is at Rose Manor."

"And?" Christina shrugged.

"Not only will she freak out when people start flashing into the kitchen but as far as she knows you're dead, remember."

"Oh yeah. Isabella goes first."

Richard turned and addressed the whole group.

"All right people the plan is Isabella will flash first with Claire and her little group. We will give her ten minutes to calm our daughter before the rest of you flash. Christina, Mattias and Jessica will flash into the kitchen. Everyone else is to flash into the back garden. There will be more room when the house sorts itself out to accommodate for everyone. Martouf and Trixie will keep check on this end while Jordan, Loki and I are….” The scared looks on the younger-one’s faces gave him pause. “Going on our own adventure to the winter palace,” he finished.

Richard walked up to Isabella and crouched down in front of the children she would be flashing with. “Now kids, Rose Manor is a magical house. While you are there I want you to find all the secret passages and rooms. Can you do that?” The children’s heads in front of him were bobbing frantically giving him his answer. Standing he placed a kiss to Isabella’s forehead. “Good luck with Janice.”

“Thanks,” Isabella said as she looked down at the two children that held her hand. The others were holding onto her arms. “Now are we ready to magically disappear?”

Smiling at the enthusiastic nodding of heads she continued. “After three. One…. Two…” Flash.

Chapter Forty-Three

Janice sat at the kitchen table going through the old books that had been left behind when her parents had gone. She didn't recall any of these stories from her childhood, but then her grandmother had told so many she was sure she must have forgotten some of them.

She glanced out the back and could clearly see her daughters still sitting on the blanket with her sister's dogs. Her two-year-old Emily was sharing her chocolate spread sandwich with the larger of the two Alsatians. She couldn't recall which one was Fane and which one was Decebel. She still enjoyed making fun of her sister over the names, she had also read those books.

Reading the book 'Prince Jordan of the Elves', Janice had a déjà vu feeling wash over her. It was like she was reading a scene from her actual life. The same night, she had in fact, met her husband Scott. A shiver ran through her and something caught her eye.

Her mother was standing by the kitchen counter. It startled her so much she stood suddenly sending the chair tumbling backwards with her still on it. She felt the pain shoot through her head as she hit the marble floor. The backrest of the chair jarred her shoulder blades.

"Janice," Isabella screeched as she ran over to her daughter. "Are you all right?"

"No," Janice said holding the back of her head and wincing in pain. She let her mother help her up and glanced at the group who had accompanied her.

"How the hell?"

"Janice, I only have ten minutes to explain this before more people arrive, your Nan included…. Oh you were reading the book on your brother," she said spotting the book Janice was still holding.

Alysha picked that moment to come in from the garden. "Nanny!" she screamed and jumped up and down, before running into Isabella's waiting arms.

"Hello munchkin," Isabella said placing a kiss on her head. "I have brought you some new friends who will be staying a few days. How about you take them into the lounge room and watch some cartoons?"

"Okay," Alysha whispered. She headed over to one of the smaller children who had only now all taken on human form. She grabbed the little girls hand and led her into the other room. The other children followed with eyes full of wonder.

Isabella watched as the last of the children left the room. "Claire, would you mind making up some snacks for the kids while we wait for the rest to get here. Where's Emily?"

"Out in the garden feeding the dogs her lunch," Janice replied. "Mother what the hell is going on?"

"Okay let me give you the quick version. Rose Manor is magical. The mirrors are portals and you are actually part Witch, Fae and Elf. You have been given Uncle Theodore's role of Guardian of the Realms. You do have your own powers from your ancestry but being the guardian you will have any of the powers when they are required. Your dad is King of the Elves and is currently making plans to go to battle against his younger brother who wants to be king. So basically your dad and brother are in danger and there will be over a hundred children turning up in a matter of minutes."

"I'm going to get Emily before she catches a cold," Janice said as she headed for the back door.

Isabella looked at Claire who was still making sandwiches. "I think that could have gone better."

"Probably," Claire replied shrugging.

"Let's get these sandwiches into the kids before the others arrive," Isabella suggested grabbing a large plate.

"Right behind you," Claire announced. "Is that Super Ted I can hear?"

Isabella glanced over her shoulder and replied, "That it is, its Alysha's favourite."

Janice watched from the back door as her mother left the room. She was feeling numb and it wasn't from the cold. She turned to where her daughters had been eating and her brows rose in surprise at the site before her. She wished she had her camera with her. Her little two-year-old had fallen asleep between the two big Alsatians. Decebel was wrapped around her and she was using Fane as a neck pillow. All of them looked rather snug and the dogs were clearly keeping Emily warm.

She could hear snarling from the dogs the closer she got to her daughter until the boys lifted their heads and saw it was her. Fane moved allowing Janice room to get her daughter. She picked her up gently and looked down at the boys.

"Your good boys for protecting Emily. Come on, let's get you both a nice big bone." She motioned with her head at the house and the dogs got up and took off towards the door. Following with a sleeping Emily on her shoulder Janice stopped dead in her tracks just as she hit the stone patio. She could hear voices inside but it was her grandmothers' voice that had stopped her, that and her name being mentioned.

"How do you know Janice is the realm guardian?" Christina said. Her voice was slightly muffled from being inside. Janice didn't really want to eavesdrop on the conversation but she was frozen to the spot.

"Because mother," Isabella retorted, "Joanne is already dabbling in witchcraft."

"And how do you know that?"

"I sensed it and Charlotte mentioned Joanne had bought a few books."

"We have to tell your father."

"Mother, I think we have more pressing issues than letting dad know he has a protégé to train," Isabella glanced at the back door. It hadn't escaped her notice that Janice hadn't come back in yet. "I think I might have sent my daughter into shock."

"She wouldn't be the first one," Christina snorted. "Where is Janice anyway?"

"In the garden."

That brought Janice out of her momentary stupor. She glanced down at her daughter happily sucking her thumb in her sleep. Janice looked again towards the back door and could see her grandmother's face peeking out from the other side of the curtains. She looked just as Janice remembered her. Janice stumbled to the back door praying she didn't drop her daughter from the shock of it all.

Christina moved a side to let her grand-daughter in and placed a kiss on her forehead.

"Nan," Janice said giving her Nan a once over. "Didn't you die?"

"Not really. Did mum tell you about other realms?" she asked and Janice nodded. "I just went back to mine that's all. So, who is this little bundle of joy?" Christina asked.

"My youngest Emily. Alysha's in the other room."

"Did you marry a nice man?"

"Yes, Scott is a wonderful husband and father."

"Soul mate," Isabella chimed in.

"What!" Christina and Janice said in unison as they turned towards her.

Isabella grabbed the family tree scroll and held it out to them.

"Would you like me to put the little one to bed?" Claire asked.

"Yes please," Janice said handing Emily over. She then took the scroll her mother held, moved a few books out of the way and placed it flat out on the table. "Who's Mattias?"

"That would be me."

Janice turned to find a handsome man in black standing next to her sister. "Mum does this mean what I think it means?"

Isabella looked at what her daughter was pointing at. "Yes it does dear."

"Okay then," she said as she turned back to Mattias. "Welcome to the family, I guess."

"What!" Mattias and Jessica said at the same time.

"You two are soul mates. Deal with it," Janice said. She was waving her hand in their direction but not once taking her eyes from the scroll. "Mum?"

"Yes sweetheart."

"How can Charlotte be pregnant?"

"What!" Jessica bolted over to the table almost knocking both her mother and sister flying.

"Dear god please don't say it's that arseholes baby."

"What arsehole?" Janice enquired.

"Dad's brother."

"Well the tree clearly states that Jordan's the father," Janice said pointing to his name.

"You should have more faith in your best friend."

"We have to tell him," Jessica stated looking at her mother.

"You can't."

"But he has to know," Jessica pleaded.

"Jessica. Your brother is not in the right emotional or mental state to be told something like that right now," Isabella said sternly.

"But—"

"No buts. Since Jordan and Charlotte haven't actually done anything physical yet he will assume that it's Vincent's baby."

"How is she pregnant then?" Janice asked in confusion.

"She was basically drugged," Isabella stated. She was still angry at her father.

"Jordan would never do such a thing," Janice said protesting at the suggestion.

"It wasn't Jordan,' Isabella said rolling her eyes. Her daughter would automatically think that she meant her brother. Pride swelled within her at how defensive and protective her children were of each other.

"Who then?"

"Your grandfather gave both Jordan and Charlotte a powerful, power-enhancing sleeping draft."

"So grand-dad isn't dead either?"

"No dear," Christina said patting Janice's arm tenderly.

"What about Uncle Theodore?" she asked sadly. She had always been close to him and it had devastated her when he died.

"What about him?" Christina said. She stopped patting Janice's arm at the mention of her son.

"Is Uncle Theodore actually dead or in another realm?" Janice said with a glimmer of hope in her voice.

"Uncle Theodore did actually pass away," Christina said mournfully.

Janice yanked her arm out from under her grandmothers as a new wave of grief washed over her.

"Why the hell is he actually dead and you're not?" Janice screeched. When she saw the horrified look on her grandmother's face, guilt consumed her. "Nanny, I'm so sorry. I didn't mean it the way it sounded."

"I know sweetheart," she whispered. Christina instantly pulled Janice into her arms and she sobbed her heart out on her shoulder. She gently rubbed the back of her head to comfort her. "You have to be happy that Uncle Theodore is back together with Aunty Beatrice and Cousin Shannon."

Christina sat on one of the kitchen chairs and perched Janice on her lap. Janice had been Theodore's favourite niece. Most likely because Janice and Shannon had been the same age. As she rubbed Janice's back Christina looked towards her daughter.

"Isabella, can we start getting everyone organised please?" Isabella nodded and started to make a move by clapping her hands and barking orders. "Mattias and Jessica. You have been given orders and I suggest you continue with fulfilling them because we don't have much time."

"Yes Nan," said Jessica placing a kiss on her grandmother's forehead. Then she placed one on her sister's head and flashed from the room.

Grabbing a handkerchief from the pocket of her silver gown she lifted Janice's head, dabbing at her tears. "Now enough of these tears. You have a very important job just like Uncle Theodore did. You're—"

"Guardian of the Realms, yeah mum told me."

"Yes, you are. When all the unpleasantness in the Elvin Realm are sorted, I will show you the beautiful Realm of the Fae." Janice just nodded because she didn't know what else to do. "Right now, up you pop. Nanny has a few pick-ups to do."

Janice stood and watched in amazement as her grandmother disappeared. A tug on her jeans brought her attention back to her oldest daughter. "What is it sweetheart?"

"Mummy, the mirror is funny."

"What do you mean the mirror is funny?"

"Come see," Alysha said grabbing her mother's hand and leading her into the lounge room.

"Oh dear," Janice said stopping in her tracks once she hit the lounge room. Alysha was pointing at the massive mirror that sat over the fire place. It could have easily at that moment been a scene of a storm playing on the television. That was the only way Janice could describe what she was now witnessing. Dark grey clouds were swirling around the glass. "Mother!" she yelled.

Isabella came running in from the kitchen after another drop off. "What is it? Oh, that can't be good."

"Well that's the last of the kids," Christina said heading down the hall towards them. "Oh, and Richard is-" Christina stopped at the door when she noticed the mirror. "That's not good."

"Mother, what's happening?" Isabella asked.

"Honestly. I haven't got a clue." Isabella and Janice turned and looked at her in shock. "Don't give me that look."

"Has this ever happened before?" Isabella asked.

"Might have?" Christina said and turned to head back into the kitchen. Isabella and Janice followed close behind. Alysha had gone back to watching cartoons and eating chocolate. She must have sneaked it past her mother in her shocked state.

"What do you mean might have?" Isabella spat. Janice was surprised at her mother's tone. She has never heard her sound so harsh.

"You watch your tone, young lady," Christina said pointing her finger at her daughter. "I don't care how old you are or what situation we currently find ourselves in you will not speak to me like that." Christina gave her daughter a stern look.

"Sorry," Isabella murmured feeling like a ten-year-old. "Mum, what are you doing?"

Christina stopped riffling through the books on the table.

"Nothing now, I found it," she said holding up the book.

"The Battle of the Realms. How is that going to explain what is going on with the mirrors?" Isabella asked in confusion.

"Janice darling, could you put the kettle on and make a cuppa please." Janice nodded and made her way through a small crowd to the kettle.

"Mother do we have time for a cuppa?"

"Has the Call of the Rose been set off?" Christina asked with raised eyebrows.

"No."

"Right then, we have time."

"Thank god, I could use a cuppa," Isabella stated slumping in a chair next to the table.

"Yes, that Elvin tea is just horrid," Christina added with a shudder, taking her own seat next to her daughter.

Janice returned with three mugs of tea and handed them out before taking her own seat.

"That was quick dear," Christina said nodding her thanks.

"Claire set up the tea urn. Nan, what's with the book?" she said motioning with her head to the book her grandmother was holding.

"Well considering our current situation in the Elvin Realm, I presumed if the mirrors had done this before it would have been during The Battle of the Realms."

"When did that happen?" Janice asked.

"Many moons ago, Uncle Theodore was a wee nipper of five at the time. He had been sent here with his big sister and—"

"But mum's younger?" Janice interrupted.

"Janice darling, your mother is not the only daughter I've had."

"Oh."

"Now. Theodore was sent here with his big sister Constance and your dad's little sister Trixie. Yes, before you ask your Dad has a sister." Christina looked at Isabella with a puzzled expression. "Why do the children not know about their Dad's siblings?" Isabella just shrugged at her mother.

"You have to raise your next batch of kids like we did you."

Isabella stared at her mother. "Yes darling, I know. Richard kind of gave it away to anyone paying enough attention. That and it's in the tree." She pointed to the spot on the family tree. "So, Jayden hey? You couldn't have picked a different letter this time around?"

"Mother, the mirrors."

"What?" Christina answered absentmindedly. Something on the tree had caught her attention.

"Why have the mirrors got storms in them?" Isabella prompted.

"Probably because of the uneasiness in the realms that Vincent is causing," Christina said looking at her daughter. "And you know what?" she said with anger in her voice.

"What?" Isabella asked wearily.

"If your sister had just done as she was bloody told," Christina said as she stood from her chair. "None of this would be happening now," she yelled throwing the book across the room in anger.

"Mum?" Isabella said as she stood up to hug her mother. She had never seen her like this.

"Vincent used to be a loving and caring soul. Constance's death totally destroyed him." A tear tracked down Christina's cheek at the memories flooding her mind. "You think your Richard is kind. He is nothing compared to how Vincent once was. If he knew that Constance had been pregnant when she was killed…. Oh, my god," Christina covered her mouth with her hand trying to hold back the tears. Why had she never known that?

"Mum, Vincent has always been kind to me. Don't forget we were once friends."

"Yeah then you married Richard," Christina said tapping her daughter's cheek.

"So?"

"You look a lot like your sister, Vincent may have thought he had his Constance back. You have been the only person that Vincent has been himself with since Constance's death. I also expect that if you faced him on the battle ground he would sooner die than have anything happen to you."

"He won't harm me but tries to kill my children?"

"Your children are also half Richard's with whom he blames for your sister's death."

"What did Richard do?"

"Nothing, which was the point. Vincent forgets that the Elves were not meant to be in the battle in the first place. However, those on the other side got greedy and ambushed the elves which nearly wiped them out."

"So how did Constance end up in a battle? If she had been brought here?"

"I would assume she had sensed her twin David being injured and flashed to him. She was the only healer born to the Fae in hundreds of years. The enemy snuck up behind her while she was healing her brother. Before either Richard or Vincent knew what was happening it was too late. Richard couldn't attack the enemy because his brother had automatically started running towards her and was in Richard's line of fire."

Christina could feel vibrating in her pocket and grabbed her gemmed communicator and opened it. "Richard. We were just talking about you."

"You ladies had better get back. We have movement in the trees," Richard ordered.

"Will do. Give us a minute."

"Tell Janice and the babies I love them all lots and that I'm sorry for dropping this on her."

"I can hear you Dad. You owe me a really expensive Christmas present for this," Janice said with a smirk although she didn't really mean it.

"Right-O sweetheart," Janice heard her Father reply before he severed the connection.

"Well looks like we had better get back. Janice my darling, I will see you again soon," Christina said as she flashed from the room before Janice could even form a reply.

"Well, you heard your father," Isabella said placing a kiss on her daughter's head. "If you have any concerns the books will tell you what's going on. I love you." she said and flashed before Janice had a chance to respond.

"What a strange day this is," Janice muttered and she made her way to the lounge room.

She now had over one hundred children to sort out.

Chapter Forty-Four

Isabella arrived in the courtyard of the main castle in the Elvin realm. It looked to be in utter chaos. People were hustling around like there was no tomorrow. For some of them there, that could very well be true. She spotted Richard and headed in his direction.

"Ah Isabella," Richard said as he placed a kiss to her forehead. He knew it was her running her arm up his shoulder before he even looked. "Where's your Mother?"

Isabella opened her mouth to answer but was cut off by the voice of his mother-in-law.

"I'm here, keep your hair on," Christina muttered making her way to the tactical table. "Richard, why is this out here?"

"There are too many people who need to see it at once. They wouldn't have all fitted in the war room," Richard said while scowling at his mother-in-law. "Besides it's a lovely afternoon and we will be able to see should anyone come near."

"Through the castle wall? You're good." Christina looked around the court yards high walls and gates.

"Oh, shut up," Richard said shaking his head slightly. "We have men up in the battlements and placed at the gates. If we were to suddenly get a surprise attack we are at least on the ground to counteract it."

Christina just shrugged. She knew she shouldn't be winding him up at a time like this. "So what's the plan?"

"Well since we don't know where the fight is going to take place there isn't one as yet. There are approximately twenty shifters in the forest close to the autumn castle on the winter palace side. Whether these are just scout groups or the first barrage is as yet, unknown."

"So, we are just leaving them alone for the moment?"

"Yes, if they are the scout group then I want to give them the impression that our defences are weak. It doesn't seem like they have spotted any of the archers we have hidden in the trees."

"You have deliberately made the courtyard look like it's in chaos," Isabella stated. She was impressed.

"Yep. If they come to the gate and have a look that is what they will see. However, it is an organised chaos and we have people strategically placed. So, if they come through the gate that's as far as they'll be getting. It is a shame that Jordan and Jessica don't know how to use their witch side."

"Why?" Christina and Isabella asked at once.

"Because those with mixed blood will be our secret weapons."

"Excuse me," Isabella said raising her brow at her husband not sure if she should be insulted or not. "Secret weapon?"

"Don't give me that look. It makes perfect sense."

"Care to enlighten me how?"

"Let's take you for example. When they see you they will think you are nothing but a measly human until you zap them with your Fae powers. It will be the same with Jordan and Jessica. Except they have a better advantage because they have elf powers too."

"Yeah all right you made your point. So what do you plan to do with these secret weapons?"

"Well, I figured we will have witches along the border of the forest," Richard said as he pinpointed it on the tactical table. "With a few who have mixed blood. So, while the witches are doing chants and things to protect the castle, those that get near the others can zap them."

"Let me guess, that's where I'm going to be," Isabella said narrowing her eyes at her husband when he smiled at her. Yep that's exactly where she was going to be. She just didn't know if it was because she was pregnant and he wanted her out of harm's way or it was because of the fact that she suited his battle plans.

"Yes, my love." Richard smiled at his wife and placed a kiss on top of her head. "We should get some men to guard the human portal and head to the neutral realm to guard the mirrors, just in case. We have no idea how far Vincent is willing to go."

"I shouldn't worry about the portals at Rose Manor," Isabella said.

"Why?" Richard said with a raised brow.

"They seem to have a storm brewing in them so I doubt anyone will be getting through that way," Isabella said blankly. "Besides, if they make it through the main portal they would have to find Rose Manor without getting arrested venturing through London with weapons. So I wouldn't worry too much about that."

"You know…" Richard said as he glanced around the court yard then back to the tactical map. "This would be so much easier if I was actually a warrior king."

"Why not ask our son for his opinion?" Isabella noticed that her son wasn't actually at the table. "Where is Jordan?"

"Over there sulking." Richard said as he lifted his arm and motioned in the direction of his son.

Isabella looked over to where her son was sitting against a wall, his arms resting on his raised knees. He was far from sulking and it annoyed her that Richard thought he was.

"Sulking my arse."

"What?" Richard said in confusion.

"Our son is not sulking. What is it about this realm? As soon as you come back you stop taking notice of your children," she said as she made to leave.

"Isabella…wait." Richard grabbed for her arm but she wriggled out of his way.

"I don't want to hear it." She glared at him before making her way over to their son. She stopped in front of him, her figure casting a shadow over him. She waited until he looked up at her.

"Hey Mum." Jordan said as he continued to pull the petals off a yellow rose.

"What's the matter?" she asked.

"Nothing," he said looking up at her and thankful that she was blocking the sun.

"Liar." Isabella sat next to him mimicking his position. "Tell mummy what's wrong."

Jordan tilted his head and cocked one of his eyebrows at her. "Mummy? Really."

"What? It's okay for you to use the mummy card and I can't when I am the mummy?"

"Fair call," Jordan shrugged.

"So," she said as she nudged his arm with hers. "Tell mummy what's wrong."

"God, I don't know? Everything, nothing." Feeling frustrated Jordan threw the rose on the ground next to him. "I just feel numb."

"Are you worried about the upcoming battle?" Isabella didn't actually think he was but felt compelled to ask.

"What's to worry about?" Jordan said as he looked straight ahead at nothing in particular. "A psycho that wants to become King is threatening to end mine and my father's life and will go to any lengths to see that is done. I'm only going to be fending off those who are hell bent on ending my life, why would I be worried. I won't go down without a fight. I would rather Vincent fight me himself, we are evenly matched and—"

"Evenly matched?" Isabella placed her hand on his forearm when he looked at her. "Sweetheart, how are you evenly matched when he is a full Elf and you are not?"

"That's why. My other abilities give me an advantage. It doesn't make me stronger with my powers but for him to gain the same abilities he has to use some of his power to get it." Jordan said shrugging. "Physically I can kick his arse."

"So, what are you worried about if not the battle?"

"Getting to Charlotte. Trixie said I would be the only one who could save her and yet I can't get anywhere near her."

"Well going in all guns blazing is a sure way to get yourself killed as you almost found out."

"I don't care about that as long as she is saved," Jordan said looking his mother in the eye. "I would die for her if I had too."

"Oh, I know that," Isabella said bluntly. "You almost have on more than one occasion."

"When?" Jordan scrunched his brows together.

"You don't remember?"

"No."

"As much as I love Charlotte, one of her greatest flaws is her bloody tunnel vision. When she was little, she ran into the road when she saw an ice cream van as most kids did. She almost got hit by a car and would have had you not suddenly appeared out of nowhere and grabbed her. You didn't look either and almost got yourself hit. So on more than one occasion you have been there to save her. I would assume that this would be no different."

"What are you saying?"

"I'm saying that when the time comes for you to save her, you will." Martouf suddenly charging across the court yard caught her attention. "Come on. Looks like something is happening."

She stood and put her hand in the crock of his elbow, helped her son up and they made their way over to the king.

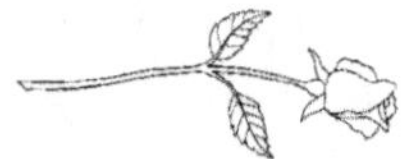

"Mattias go and get Trixie and the other women," Richard ordered as he spotted Martouf charging towards him. This couldn't be good.

"Yes your Majesty."

Mattias flashed just as Martouf got to Richard.

"Richard," Martouf said breathlessly. He was breathing too heavily to get his breath back so he leant on Richards arm and tried to slow the breaths he was taking. "Richard, we have movement. The attack has started."

"How do you know that?" Richard asked as Martouf regained his composure.

"One of the fae spies contacted Lampros—"

"I didn't know Lampros knew any fae spies."

"You'll be surprised exactly who my cousin knows."

"Fair enough, so what's happening?"

"It's started. There is an army of about two hundred headed this way."

"My brother?"

"He is leading the attack."

"And Charlotte?"

"She has been left at the castle. However, it is unknown as to how many guard her if any."

"Well, we will have to assume that she is safe for now. Unless she does something stupid."

"She wouldn't do anything, would she?" Martouf frowned.

"You don't know Charlotte," Richard said rubbing his chin. "Stubborn as an ox and balls of steel when needed that one."

"WHAT THE HELL are they wearing?" Martouf almost screeched.

Richard turned and saw his daughter, sister and a couple of Elvin women dressed in a short leather outfit that was too revealing for his liking. He couldn't miss the scowl on Mattias' face.

"What do ya think?" Trixie asked while doing a twirl before facing him.

"I don't know what to think." Richard just stared at his sister and noticed that all the men were doing the same. "There's an easy kill," he muttered.

"That's the point," Trixie said catching what he said. "The bodice is layered with bone to give it an armoured effect," she said running her hands down her torso.

"And the plunging neck line?"

Trixie groped her chest and adjusted her breasts. "Using our natural gifts and by the looks of that lot it works a treat. The split skirt is to aid with movement."

"And a belt to attach the weapons too," Richard observed as he glanced over his daughter's attire. "You watch too much tele," he added pointing at her.

"What? It also has a breast knife in it." She pulled out a knife that's handle matched the bodice design. "And a hair one too." She bent her head and pointed to something that resembled a hair comb.

Richard looked at Martouf. "I hate to say this but it looks like the girls are more prepared for battle than we are." Martouf nodded in agreement with his mouth still hanging open. "Right let's get this show on the road. Martouf, Mattias start gathering everyone together."

Richard waited for everyone to get assembled before he addressed the crowd and he had no idea what he was going to say, never mind anything else. He wiped the sweat from his brow and cleared his throat. The murmurs stopped instantly.

"The time has come to go into what will surely be a dangerous fight, not only for Elves but all of us here. We all know my brother is using this opportunity to try to take the throne and only the ancestors know what will happen if he succeeds. In saying that, I ask those of you that have sworn to protect the king to disregard that and concentrate on protecting the prince."

Richard could have sworn he thought he had asked them to chop their hands off from all the gasps that were heard. Never mind the fact his son was clearly upset by his request from their people. He looked like he was only staying put because his mother's hand was placed on his chest. Richard had his reasons for the request.

"Why would you ask this of us?" one elf asked bowing slightly to show his respect for the king.

"The Elves at the Winter Palace have sided with my brother and the fact that the next in line for the throne is a human has displeased them. Vincent has used this information to win them over. I will make my decision a royal decree if I must, but I am hoping I do not have to. We know that I have the ability to protect myself with a shield. My son however does not and I would ask that you protect the future king at all costs. My son is strong and will be able to hold his own even though I expect a great deal of the enemy to be focussed on him. Our main objective is to protect the prince at all costs."

"What about the girl?"

"If we lose this fight then she will be lost to us any way. Let's concentrate on one thing at a time. We will make our stand in the forest before the autumn castle. Those from the witch factions will be this side of the forest with Isabella and the others with fae blood. Those who can take up arms will do so. We will also be in mixed groups to add an element of surprise to our defence. Group leaders you know those who are in your group so start gathering your teams together. Once we hit the edge of the forest for god sake stay put, do not charge toward the castle. We will make our stand where we can be covered by the trees and wait for the enemy to make the first move. If they use powers then we use our powers. If they fight dirty, then by the ancestor's we also fight dirty. Let's move out and may the ancestors be with you."

Richard winced at Trixie's giggle, which was more like a cackle. He couldn't believe he had just done what she loved to do even if it was by accident. Grabbing his sword, quiver and bow he made his way to the castle gates. Dread filled his stomach with every step.

It hadn't taken Richard long before he found himself at the edge of the autumn forest. He had been aware of Martouf and Lantash next to him the entire way but hadn't really been paying attention to anything. He'd felt like a man on his way to the gallows and the end results could very well be the same. He'd given Isabella a kiss and told her he loved her when he passed her at the entrance of the forest.

"Déjà vu," Richard muttered as he looked at the newly restored castle. "Mattias, if things go bad here today promise me you will get my children out of this."

"I will," Mattias answered from behind Richard. He was getting himself ready to take his usual spot in the trees.

Richard looked to his other generals and close friends. Lantash had his Sai weapons out and Martouf had his hand on the hilt of his sword.

"Jessica."

"Don't worry dad I won't flash my tits to get the upper hand," she said smirking.

Richard spun his head around so fast he was surprised it hadn't spun right off. "Good god girl if it saves your life you will bloody well do it. Now I forgot what I was actually going to say," he said as he turned back to the castle. "Jordan, you ready for this?"

"Fuck no."

"You'll do fine," he snickered. "Martouf. If my children die today make sure to take me out also."

"Why?"

"Would you want to face Kynthia if Nicodemus got killed?"

"Consider it done, your Majesty."

Richards's attention was drawn back to the now gathering army in front of the castle. He could see that Vincent was anxious to get things started. They were about to see how this fight would begin and when a barrage of lightning bolts headed towards them they got their answer.

"And so, it begins," Richard said getting his shields ready.

Dear Reader,

Thank you for taking the time to read my book. I hope you have enjoyed reading it as much as I have enjoyed writing it. Please feel free to leave a review about the book, even if it's just a few words to say what you thought or who your favourite character was.

As many times as this book has been proof read, there are bound to be a couple of mistakes that have managed to slip through. If you do happen to notice anything please let me know by email at: chanellenash23@gmail.com

If you liked this book and would like to hear about future books in the series you can follow me on
Twitter: Twitter.com/chanellenash
or
Facebook: www.facebook.com/authorchanellenash

Acknowledgements
and
Notable Mentions

I would like to thank my family and friends for all their encouragement with the writing of this book.

A special thank you to Kylie, Nick and Jim and his lovely wife. You guys know what for.

In chapter four Charlotte happens to be reading a book called 'There and Now' with a character with whom she rather liked called 'Doctor Jonathan Fortner'. It is an actual book by Linda Lael Miller which I read in May 1993. I was at home sick from school and raided my Mum's romance collection. I read the book so much that I have had to tape it back together on more than one occasion and yes for those who know me, I did like Doctor Fortner as well.

Charlotte also refers to a book series which Jessica had been reading when naming her dogs and was later referenced again by Janice. This is an actual series by Quinn Loftis called The Grey Wolves series. I have read the books and personally love the series. Decebel is my favourite character in the collection.

So I would like to say a massive thank you to both Ms Miller and Ms Loftis for giving me permission to keep those references in my book.

About the Author

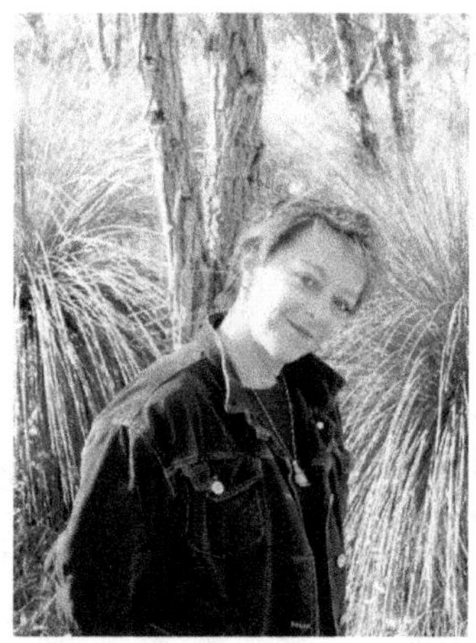

Photo courtesy of Tanya K Photography

As a child Chanelle loved to create bedtime stories for her younger siblings. She would let them pick characters and would then create a story from them.

Born in London, Chanelle moved to Australia when she was thirteen with her parents and four younger siblings and still continues to travel between the two countries.

Currently residing in Perth, Western Australia Chanelle shares a house with her youngest sibling and their dog Demetrius and cat's Smoke, Jensen & Shadow.

When not working at her part time job Chanelle can be found spending time with family and friends. Writing stories or letters, reading, doing genealogy and listening to music are also some of her favourite things to do.

Other books in
The Call of the Rose Series:

INTO THE REALM